The New Hollywood

Books by Axel Madsen

Billy Wilder
William Wyler: The Authorized Biography
The New Hollywood

THE NEW HOLLYWOOD

American Movies in the '70s

Axel Madsen

THOMAS Y. CROWELL COMPANY
New York   Established 1834

Designed by Ingrid Beckman

Manufactured in the United States of America

ISBN 0-690-00538-5

Library of Congress Cataloging in Publication Data

Madsen, Axel.
    The new Hollywood.

    1. Moving-picture industry—California—Hollywood.   I. Title.
PN1993.5.U65M26   338.4'7'791430973   74-14553
ISBN 0-690-00538-5
1   2   3   4   5   6   7   8   9   10

Contents

"It's like the killeyoo bird."

"The what?"

"You know, the killeyoo bird; it flies backwards because it doesn't care where it's going, it just wants to see where it has been."

—Clare Booth Luce

1

The State of the Art

ALMOST EVERYTHING is new in the movies—the message, the people, the significance. Contemporary Hollywood has little to do with the Southern California sex'n surf lotusland. It has less to do with the company town of the parade gone by, or even with the opulent insularity of a few decades ago. Movies in the seventies have a different resonance than they had in the mid-1950s or the high 1930s, which doesn't mean that the interaction of movies and national life isn't as intense as ever.

The vast majority who left the movies for their television sets years ago are beginning to drift back. "People are going to the movies again," says Columbia Pictures president David Begelman. "The opportunity has been given back to us."

Creators with a capital C and a sense of what goes have never had it so good. "Not forgetting all the smarmy statements I've made about Hollywood in the past, there's no pleasure in the world as great as directing a movie here," says Orson Welles. Making movies in the 1970s means splashing zap, excitement, and appeal on the screen and reflecting the hunger and needs of the junior half of the population.

Reaction to Hollywood has always been exaggerated. Declaring the Los Angeles postal zone a wasteland has been a media game since 1914 when trade papers contended the medium had exhausted its possibilities. Sixty years later, Hollywood was still there, economically holding its own while edging toward an all-media New

Dawn. Movies and, even more, moviegoers have changed. Present-day film audiences, as Stanley Kauffmann has said, are the first pop cultists who can see fourth-rate melodrama for what it is and at the same time glory in the director's use of the camera and his expertness in film mythology. An industry climbing toward $3 billion in annual worldwide earnings—and America's multinational film companies take in one-third of that—doesn't lie down but adapts itself. Hollywood studios are slimmed-down but humming work assemblies. They don't stand like Florida "spaceports" as paradigms of Instant Obsolescence. The chronicle of Hollywood in the seventies is a story of change and renewal, under pressure. Inflation and recession are not among the film industry's woes—on the contrary. The downbeat economic reality of the mid-1970s is having the same effect as the 1930s depression had; it is sending people to the movies in record numbers, presumably in search for the same escape and romance. As the world reeled under the economic multiple jeopardy, movie attendance shot up almost everywhere, and the American film industry was able to post its highest domestic boxoffice results—albeit in inflation-lightweight dollars—in nearly thirty years. Although a 1975 dollar is worth only 26 cents in 1946 currency, the projected American boxoffice take for 1974 was $1.65 billion, only some $40 million short of the 1946 all-time peak of $1.69 billion. If the recession hurt, it was in such esoteric areas as the auto manufacturers' decision to drop the practice of lending cars, cost-free, to transport Hollywood executives in exchange for on-screen exposure of the latest automotive elegance.

"The picture business is different today," says producer Jennings Lang. "We now read scripts and ask, in addition to whether it's good or not, 'Can it sell?' 'Could it be done on TV?' "

If television would want it, it's no longer for the movies. The vast majority who left the moviehouses for their television sets years ago are not coming back to the theaters to pay for what they see for free at home. "You've got to send out something more than just a can of film," says Lang. "And you've got to have stars and stories not seen on TV. And then—if you get three hits out of thirteen or fourteen films a year, you've got it made."

In practically all countries except the United States, moviemaking is financed with public funds and regarded, like a seat in the U.N., as an expression of national prestige. As a nine-to-five industry, Hollywood is unique—a highly speculative business working on the profit motive of supply and demand to a capricious and demanding clientele. There is nothing in the world quite like Hollywood—today more than ever a pool of finances and talent rather than a geographical entity, since the Hollywood "majors" are a world power. If an Argentinian, Swedish, or Czech film is to be seen on all continents, it tries to become a Warner's, Paramount, or Fox release.

The cinema is no longer *the* mass medium—television is, which doesn't mean it has lost its power to engross, as movies on TV prove. Forms, style, and meaning, however, only emerge from the big screen. Artistically, television is a mechanical device, a playback for culture reduced to ideograms. Of late, television is even getting more serious, and movies are providing more escapist entertainment.

Meanwhile the distinction between cinema and "audiovisuals" is blurring, and just over the horizon lie technical innovations which will have an enormous impact not only on the film and TV industry but on music, theater, publishing, journalism, and big business. This Third Revolution in electronics—the first two were radio and TV—will dramatically transform cultural habits and, finally, "demassify" mass communications, and in so doing produce new rules, new winners, and new losers. "Audiovision" is advance-billed as the equivalent of the paperback revolution in publishing.

With its special air of madness, moviemaking is, like politics, the art of the possible. Hollywood's natural fondness for magic formulas, plus the hit-or-miss mathematics of contemporary film business, tend to discourage innovation. But all art is, at bottom, experimental, and the bosses know it. Money is not so much a barrier to moviemaking as a limit to the *kind* of movie that gets made.

The "old" Hollywood—the place where Gloria Swanson and Humphrey Bogart used to hang out—is gone, and the only stars anyone will see on Hollywood Boulevard today are those embedded in the pink granite sidewalks. Classic Hollywood died circa 1950, and its heirs are neither the grandchildren of the Caesars and praetors nor the descendants of the stars, producers, directors, and labor aristocracy, but all the attorneys and agents of these Beautiful People. After acting so long as counselors-at-law, contract writers, tax experts, and general court jesters, the Beverly Hills "ten percenters" and attorneys have taken over corporate Hollywood.

Screenfare is its own diminishing returns. Audiences keep growing younger and better educated—selective, unpredictable, too, and often less forgiving than critics. Although the 1970 "youthquake" proved to be a dud, it is implicitly understood that the movies are a youth-oriented industry. The question everyone asks himself is, "How young do I *look* up there on the screen?" Today's America is weary of confrontation, and emotionally already light-years away from what Penelope Gilliatt has called the "brassy, swinging, ungallant taste of the sixties." Contemporary public tastes, it seems, demand a saner life-style, and people withdraw voluntarily into less public, more private forms of rebellion. Yet the movies continue to "sell" what they know best—high-adrenalin heroics, or antiheroics.

The reason is obvious. Ian Fleming was one of the few writers who could outdo the cinema and *write* a better sensation of fast driving, for example, than the movies with their screaming tires on sound tracks, close-ups of hands on the wheel, and windshield views of sucked-up asphalt. Movies work best in primary colors. Movies have always been best in blacks and whites, even if current formula flicks sentimentalize defeat and accept corruption that wipes out *moral* distinctions.

Modern screen heroes are not knights in shining armor flushing varmit from them thar hills, but good guys and bad guys in conflict and heavy chases are still what movies are made of, even if moral decay and men with frazzled, fatigued sensitivities are fashionable.

To idealists, filmmaking is not a profession but a calling, and this has made contemporary cinema very self-conscious. Cinephiles want the medium to be an ethical and metaphysical view of man, a vision encompassing all facts and values. The radical thunder of a few years ago, however, has turned into ideological indigestion, even at the Cannes film festival. Even if it is still considered bad taste to have too keen a sense of money, new directors are displaying a healthy enough appetite for commercial zap. New people coming up in Hollywood are not "angry," but dedicated and thoughtful, if somewhat intense. They are usually in their late twenties, talented and in possession of a surprising knowledge of business realities.

The medium now definitely belongs to the director. Proprietary and creative-rights clauses in collective agreements have made the "hired hand" director an anachronism. Money is raised, "packages" are put together, and actors and actresses are attracted on the director's name, personality, and "track record." The number of players whose scrawl on the bottom line sets everything in motion has dwindled to a handful, and no star is "bankable" in the sense that his or her signature is collateral for a production bank loan.

Which doesn't mean glamour and excitement aren't part of the mystery and allure of the movies. The pleasure of moviegoing is watching incandescent people on the screen, and films are still "sold" on their on-screen talent. Yet, the system is no longer star-oriented. New, electrifying actors and actresses confess to feeling lost in today's Hollywood. When they don't make jokes about their screen magic, they ally themselves with agent-producers in order to retain a measure of control over their careers and over the films they appear in.

"The newest trend is that both ends of 'talent'—director and stars—come together *before* the project gets to the studio," says Columbia executive Peter Guber. *The Fortune*, uniting Mike Nichols with Jack Nicholson and Warren Beatty around an original Carol Eastman screenplay, was such a take-it-or-leave-it royal flush of script, director, and stars that Columbia found it irresistible.

Directors and stars need each other for high-power packages. If the star system is both exploded myth and persistent reality, the director as superstar has also failed to translate into dollars-and-cents dependability. The central fact of contemporary movie life is packaging—the savant combining of script, director, and on-screen talent. Packaging is the last frontier if not the ultimate justification of the producer, who is almost always an agent, a lawyer, or an accountant upgraded to producership as a means of securing additional participation points for his clients. The situation is not ideal, because more energy is spent putting the coincidence together than getting it on film, but it has ultimately worked to the director's advantage. Agents, lawyers, and accountants have a limited grasp of actual filmmaking and their active involvement tends to end with the first day's shooting. A growing number of studio bosses, however, come from the ranks of talent and literary agents.

Show business success is, like green salad, a perishable commodity, and not something that can be blueprinted and system-engineered. If it were, Hollywood would be a town of millionaires. But success can be recycled, and the only thing Hollywood really trusts is success.

Making movies is the ability to function within narrow sensory bands, to be "fine-tuned" to public attitudes. A writer and sculptor can be a decade or a century ahead of his time, a filmmaker must be right-on. Making movies is bringing together individual talents and public longings. It is dramatizing current contradictions and recognizing new myths and the element of public wish-fulfillment that is essential in any filmic success.

Making movies is a feel of complicity with audiences and the ability to break through to that elusive youth market, against which so many films and fortunes have been smashed. Movies are a porous mix of intentions and happy accidents. Making movies is the ability to function inside a revolving kaleidoscope made of green cheese. Now you see it, now you don't.

For no good reason, the "majors"—Columbia Pictures, Walt Disney Productions, Twentieth Century–Fox, Paramount Pictures, Warner Brothers, United Artists, and Universal Pictures—have abdicated the "first initiative." Packagers set things in motion.

Today's film world is freer than ever, but chances are fewer. To direct a first picture is easier than it ever was; to make a fifth or a tenth movie is another story.

There is no longer any training ground. The Archie Bunker unions are trying to hang in there. Nobody is mourning their slow fade-out, but their demise means the end of traditional apprenticeship. Nearly two hundred American colleges and universities offer degrees in film and television, all turning out would-be Fellinis instead of set designers, camera operators, and sound engineers. To remain viable, the medium needs technicians and administrators, people who are esthetically aware, but who also have a business mind and can function in inflated-ego atmospheres.

New talent—both in front of and behind the camera—doesn't come from television, because the only thing the movies cannot afford is hacks. Movies have to be so much better because they are for cash. Any young Orson Welles can still walk right in.

Some things never change. To know how to hustle—an ingredient not included in academic curricula—is all-important, as it always was. The movies always attracted gifted, hungry, and crazy people and always demanded gregarious, persuasive, if not overpowering, personalities.

Despite perennial talk of "independent filmmaking," outside money remains negligible. Getting a film to market means dealing with one of the "majors," and their grip is tightening. The reason is that production, financing, and distribution are irrevocably linked, and it is terribly expensive to get a movie to the world's screens. To survive, the majors quite simply combine diversified risk taking with international marketing.

"Thirty years ago, movies competed with each other; today they compete with TV, tennis, camping, golf, and macramé," says Guber. "We've come to realize that the price of a movie ticket must be figured in relation to people's time, not to their money. To most people, the question is not so much whether it costs $2.50 or $3.50 to see a movie, but whether that movie is worth anybody's two and a half hours."

Bringing a picture to the screen *is* very expensive. A sobering fact of life is that only forty cents of each dollar clunked down at the boxoffice goes back to the movie's distributor, and that only fifteen cents is actually available for negative costs (the costs up to the first completed print of the film before advertising and distribution charges are added), the rest being swallowed up in overheads and profits.

The movies were born hermaphrodite—half art and half lucre. The cinema never lived on its masterpieces but between them, and, as Hollywood approaches its seventy-fifth anniversary, that is, again, the ongoing event. What is new in the mid-1970s is the economic reality, with money the unlikely ally of sanity, quality, and a certain forward thrust. As the United States lumbers toward a trillion-dollar economy (a near-metaphysical concept, a one followed by twelve zeros), the film industry is jogging right along. Taking in $1.6 billion at home, another $1 billion or so in the rest of the world, and another $500 million from television, it tops the pet food industry in the United States, the GNP of Kenya or Chile, and Argentina's total annual exports.

Since its gold rush, the world has looked to California for tall yarns. Hollywood's extravagant drama is an intrigue of passion and money that Balzac—and Ernst Lubitsch—would have savored.

2

The View from the Top

"People who go around saying Hollywood is dead amuse me," says Lew Wasserman with a smile, in his office suite high up in the Universal glass tower. "If what they say is so, then how come we've got $20 million worth of film-related construction going on here?"

Lew Wasserman is the most powerful man in the film business, a stringlike silhouette of an executive who rises at five o'clock in the morning and spends his evenings screening features and TV shows in his Beverly Hills mansion. He is gracious and softspoken and is considered to be one of the most aggressive men in a business full of aggressive men. He rarely surfaces on the public record, opting instead for an occasional picture on the society pages. He has been married to the same woman for forty years and thinks "ruthless" is an outmoded word. "I don't think our society today permits people to be ruthless," he says. "As for being hard, yes, I guess I'm guilty."

Three months after he married Edith Beckerman he landed a job as national advertising manager of Music Corporation of America, a talent-booking agency founded by Jules Stein, a Viennese who was also a composer on the schmaltzy side of his own definition. Wasserman was twenty-two and more tempted by the high-sounding title than the $60-a-week salary. "The job has a great future," he told his bride. "Stein is forty. He's an old man." When Stein turned fifty, he named Wasserman president. Together they built

MCA, Inc., into a vast entertainment empire, expanding from talent agency to moviemaker until Attorney General Robert Kennedy brought antitrust action to force them to divorce talent handling from production work. In compliance, MCA chose to leave the agency business and to cast its lot with production. In 1969, when conglomerate swallow-ups were the craze of Wall Street, MCA was only inches away from becoming a division of Firestone Tires.

"Lew was very mature and thoughtful at twenty-two," says Edith. "He never did anything foolish."

Wasserman, who since 1973 has been MCA's chairman, is at pains to appear modest. "I'm just a paper pusher," is his description of his $250,000-a-year job. For the past decade, his influence has been felt throughout the industry because he has also been the chairman of the Association of Motion Picture and Television Producers (AMPTP). The title may smack of chamber of commerce good deeds, but AMPTP is in fact the all-powerful management body which, among other things, bargains with unions representing upwards of 40,000 film industry workers. In 1973 Wasserman was heavily involved with union negotiations, and a deciding factor in the settlement of a lengthy writers' strike.

Universal is making money—lots of it. The good fortunes began in 1972 with *Pete'n Tillie*, continued with *High Plains Drifter* and *Day of the Jackal*, then grew still more with *Jesus Christ Superstar* and the unexpected runaway hit *American Graffiti*, plus *The Sting*. In 1974, Universal reported record-breaking six-month earnings of $25.2 million on revenues of $306 million, and theatrical film production was at a ten-year high.

MCA, Inc., owns the biggest and busiest movie studio in the world—Universal. "Yes, I've made mistakes," Wasserman admits. "I tend to forget about them, however. With the volume of production our company is involved in, errors of judgment about an individual film or TV show are inevitable. On any project you have only a certain amount of time to make your best judgment and take your sharpest aim at the target."

MCA not only keeps all of its sound stages and 6,000 employes busy but makes a highly profitable sideshow out of the studio, running herds of tourists around the 400-acre backlot to show them how movies are made. Although the company has a reputation of being the most cost-conscious company in the business, it is not rigid about budgets. The stress is on selecting the right projects and fitting the budget to the needs of the film. Wasserman has an insatiable appetite for facts. "Why this subject? What's the logic behind it? What are we trying to achieve? What's the point of view? Where is the preproduction planning? How will it be executed?" are frequent questions for Wasserman, who is fed hourly bulletins on how Universal pictures are doing at the boxoffice. The studio maintains a seven-day-a-week "code-a-phone" spewing statistics on opening engagements of specific films all over the world to company executives. Wasserman himself receives the first reports on the number of people buying tickets to specific films at 5:00 A.M. (8:00 A.M. New York time). He constantly reappraises market approaches.

What disturbs Wasserman most is seeing critics scold Universal for not giving enough time, effort, love, patience, and money to its films. "It's simply not true; all our pictures are given time, effort, love, patience, and money. We watch all features closely in their first one hundred to one hundred and fifty engagements. Wherever a film opens, we can tell on a daily basis how much money that film has grossed. Nevertheless, that's one area where all companies, including ours, could stand improvement. Many good films never penetrate the market."

If Wasserman feels MCA's marketing approach is wrong, advertising and distribution patterns are reexamined and sometimes a booking is canceled. Wasserman did that with *Slaughterhouse Five*, initially booked into the so-called keys—big city markets. When customers stayed away in droves, Wasserman's braintrust decided the George Roy Hill adaptation of the Kurt Vonnegut best seller had a chance with college audiences. *Slaughterhouse Five* was taken out of the "keys" and opened in smaller college towns—Ann Arbor instead of Detroit, Austin instead of Dallas. The film caught on with college audiences and was moved back into the cities.

When Wasserman moved upstairs to become chairman of MCA, he named Sidney Sheinberg president. The thirty-nine-year-old Sheinberg had been head of Universal-TV, perhaps its most powerful division.

"In its heyday, Metro-Goldwyn-Mayer, which was probably the biggest and best of the studios during the 1930s and 40s, produced one hundred hours of film a year," says Wasserman. "Today, we make three hundred hours of film at Universal and spend more than any two or three studios spent in those heydays combined." By hours of film, Wasserman means Universal's output for both big and little screens. "You must realize that the cost of one hour of television film today is higher than the total cost of an old MGM Andy Hardy film, or for that matter the Ma and Pa Kettle movies we made here.

"Movie buffs tend to be as ignorant about the movie industry as they are knowledgeable about its products. The business is changing and obviously will keep changing as people get more affluent and have more leisure time."

The adapting has been going strong since the late 1960s, with various firing squads occupying center stage and a cast of thousands disappearing into the wings.

The spate of corporate mergers which made movies a fringe operation of Big Business diminished in the 1970s in the face of sobering experiences at the boxoffice and changed fiscal policies in Washington. Ironically, the reasons for the sellouts were less mismanagement than the innate flimsiness of movies as negotiable goods, combined with the deeper involvement in European production, which demanded forever heavier outlays of cash. Paramount Pictures became a division of Gulf & Western Industries, a vastly diversified insurance company trust. United Artists sold out to Transamerica Corporation of San Francisco, a service company originating in Bank of America. After merging with the largely Canadian holding company of Seven Arts Productions, Warner Brothers became a subsidiary of Kinney National (parking lots, funeral parlors, auto rentals, and *Mad* and eighteen other magazines). After changing its name to Kinney Services the whole conglomerate, which also includes Atlantic Records, Panavision, and several cable TV companies, named itself Warner Communications, Inc. Joseph E. Levine's lively little Embassy Pictures came under the Avco umbrella (military and space hardware, banking, and Carte Blanche), leaving MCA, Columbia Pictures, and the family-owned and vastly diversified Disney organization the only majors still in moviemakers' control.

After three years of proxy battles, MGM went through three management changes in one year. Finally, Las Vegas financier (and former airline pilot) Kirk Kerkorian took command in 1969 by purchasing 40 percent of Metro for $80 million, and for four years he had former CBS president James Aubrey liquidate the once-proud Tiffany of Hollywood. The decline and fall of MGM was neither inevitable nor unavoidable. Kerkorian and Aubrey sold $62 million of company assets—everything from faded movie props to a record and music publishing subsidiary—and plowed the money into the $110 million MGM Grand Hotel in Las Vegas. "From now on the company that brought you *Ben Hur* and *The Wizard of Oz* will bring you crap—and roulette, slot machines and all the other pleasures of a Las Vegas casino hotel," *Forbes* magazine wrote in October 1973, when for all intents and purposes MGM ceased to exist as a producer-distributor of theatrical films. A month later, Aubrey himself was dismissed and replaced by Frank E. Rosenfelt, a former lawyer whose first job was to try and restore credibility by saying the MGM lion still roared.

Rosenfelt, who joined the industry at Radio-Keith-Orpheum (RKO) before shifting to Metro in 1955, "appears to be a man who wants to run a company by hiring talent instead of hiring, then second-guessing, talent," *Variety* commented on his appointment.[1] His first slate, however, looked no better than Aubrey's: a Dean Martin yarn, *Ricco*, directed by Paul Bogart, and Herbert Ross's cinematization of Neil Simon's *The Sunshine Boys* were his first productions, to be followed by *Futureworld* (a sequel to *Westworld*, but without the input of Michael Crichton), *The All-American Girl*, and *Guns*.

During his four years as Metro's $208,000-a-year studio boss, Aubrey cut employment from 6,200 to 1,200, slashed debts, and put the company back in the black with such medium-budget schlock as *Skyjacked*, *Soylent Green*, and *The Man Who Loved Cat Dancing*, but he rubbed creative people the wrong way. His heavy involvement in creative detail far surpassed his immersion in CBS scripts, when his chilling heartlessness had first earned him the nickname "the smiling cobra," but it earned him nothing but enemies and lawsuits. Aubrey's involvement translated into the ultimate humiliation for directors—substantial alterations of their vision, the changing of films and their subsequent exploitation. It started with Robert Altman and *Brewster McCloud*. "Altman was totally mistreated," said producer Lou Adler.

Aubrey locked Paul Magwood out of the cutting room on *Chandler*, cut twenty-one minutes from *Going Home* behind Herbert Leonard's back, insulted Blake Edwards in front of cast and crew on *A Case of Need*, and re-edited Sam Peckinpah's *Pat Garrett and Billy the Kid* and Ken Russell's *The Boy Friend*. "I got my two cuts, the second was approved by vice-president Herb Solow," Jack Smight said of *The Traveling Executioner*. "Then Aubrey went to

1. *Variety*, Nov. 7, 1973.

work. I was stunned. He recut it with a lawn mower." [2] Two MGM pictures—the only two to do very well at the boxoffice—were not protested. One, David Lean's *Ryan's Daughter*, was already completed when Aubrey took over, and Lean reportedly had a contract which no one dared violate. The other was Gordon Parks' *Shaft*. The black detective story got through because Parks convinced Aubrey he knew the black audience and Aubrey didn't. "The Kerkorian-Aubrey management of MGM," wrote Vincent Canby when it was all over, "was the realization of everyone's worst fears of what would happen to Hollywood when the money-men take over." [3]

Filmmaking has always tempted the wealthy, and "new money" has never been in short supply in the high-risk glamour business. Short-lived incursions have been such network stabs at filmmaking as ABC Pictures and Cinema Center Films (CBS), which, ineptly, produced little except *Little Big Man* and lots of red ink. Other ventures were themselves conglomerate film-industry spinoffs and diversifications inside the "leisure upmarket"—into publishing (RCA), hotels (MGM and, for a while, Columbia), real-estate (Fox), and electronics (MCA). The game is international. Holland's mighty N. Z. Philips corporation and Britain's Anglo-EMI, itself the result of corporate consolidations, were in and out of the sweepstakes; Gulf & Western's horizons went beyond Paramount, Dot Records and Famous Music. Reader's Digest went into partnership with United Artists on *Tom Sawyer* and *Huckleberry Finn*. Fabergé, Inc., bankrolled eight uneven, slightly old-fashioned pictures, Playboy Enterprises sank big money into a Roman Polanski version of *Macbeth* and a film based on Desmond Morris' book *The Naked Ape*, and such upstarts as Britain's Visual Programs Systems and Goodtime Enterprises have managed to get Rothschild money behind them in ventures aimed for 1980, when movies, television ("on air," pay, cable), and videocassettes are supposed to melt into one orgiastic, all-media never-never land.

Together with D. W. Griffith and Charles Chaplin, Mary Pickford and her husband, Douglas Fairbanks, Sr., founded United Artists in 1919. Fifty years later, Paul Newman, Sidney Poitier, and Barbra Streisand (in that alphabetical order) signed incorporation papers for the First Artists Production Company, Ltd. "The

2. *Los Angeles Times*, Dec. 28, 1971.
3. *New York Times*, Oct. 30, 1973.

movie industry is moving into a new era," said Poitier grandly. "You either lead it, or move with it, or follow it. We have opted for leadership."

With Steve McQueen and Dustin Hoffman joining later, First Artists' first offerings were a mixed bag. Newman's contribution, *Pocket Money*, was a bomb, and Miss Streisand's *Up the Sandbox* also ended up in the red, indicating, as *Variety* put it, "that however talented the group may be, their names alone apparently are no box office insurance." [4] While Poitier's *Warm December* was a further disappointment, McQueen's *The Getaway*, directed by Sam Peckinpah, saved the day with domestic boxoffice returns of $17.5 million (Hoffman never made *his* picture). First Artists' pictures were bankrolled and released by National General Pictures Corporation until Warner's swallowed up both operations in 1973. "It never works," said Paramount cofounder Adolph Zukor on his one-hundredth birthday that year. "You can't take a star and let him run his own business."

First Artists' foremost concern was to prove its unqualified dedication to the star system, and since its four stockholders were actors, the company was obviously primed to sympathize with actors' problems and recognize them as an important part of the filmmaking process. The *modus operandi* allowed each of the four stars to choose those projects they believed best suited their talents. And their egos. As originally conceived, *Warm December* was a triangular love story, with Poitier and Johnny Sekka vying for the affections of Esther Anderson. By the time producer-director-star Poitier delivered his final cut, most of Sekka was on the cutting room floor and *Warm December* was a Poitier-Anderson duo. The *Up the Sandbox* budget was shot when cast and crew went to Kenya for a dream sequence, with imported Senegalese dancers, that could have been shot in Griffith Park. Actors' most memorable roles are rarely in films where they have "artistic control."

After First Artists, Fabergé discovered that without a major studio tie-up guaranteeing, if not first, at least exclusive rights to its films, production is hardly worth it. Institutions that have gone into film financing and production without having control over a distribution organization have never lasted.

Although the industry enjoys a fairly generous tax regime, the Nixon administration began looking with disfavor at the growing power of conglomerates in 1972. The government refused to give in to labor pressure to put Hollywood on welfare rolls by granting export subsidies. A year later, the Internal Revenue Service tightened its rules on "venture capital" tax write-offs in film.

A combination of bad gambling and audience defection to "little" films caught Hollywood with capital investments of $100 million in 1970, and conglomerate ardor cooled. Gulf & Western put the 52-acre Paramount lot up for sale, only to have second thoughts after *The Godfather* changed the arithmetic. The two-year-long night saw American majors lose over half a billion dollars ($525 million), and for a while Hollywood did look like that tired metaphor—a ghost town. Fox, Paramount, and Warner's went into hibernation in 1970–71, as all the majors except Disney "restructured" and layoffs hit even established personnel. Fox alone fired, retired, or furloughed 2,000 studio employes.

"Everyone is probing the likely moviegoing habits in years ahead and creating films on the best guesses," Columbia's president, Leo Jaffe, said in 1972. "There is no such thing as a built-in audience today. The problem is not selling films or even making them, but knowing two years in advance what people's taste and fashion will be." Jaffe didn't read his own tea leaves right. A year and a $50 million deficit later, *he* was out.

A certain lumpen-wisdom has it that nothing really changes, that what the customer wants is sheer entertainment—"movie-movies." Boldness, originality, emotional impact, and a sure-footed deployment of the medium's resources, it is said, are what successful movies are made of. True or not, Hollywood itself is hard of learning. Less than two years after the 1970–72 debacle, the spiraling insanity of astronomical investments in untested best sellers and big-name actors and directors was again pointing film economics toward suicidal heights. "For one or two years, everybody was scaled down," American International Pictures' (AIP) president Samuel Z. Arkoff said in the fall of 1973. "But now major studios are letting themselves be sucked into the same goddamn pattern. The $750,000-to-$1-million actor that no studio wanted to pay more than $250,000 for last year is getting $750,000 again, but now, in addition, he's getting it against a piece of the gross."

Coming to terms with realities is the lesson of the 1970s. Movie executives have always hoped that their high-risk industry was becoming "rationalized," but somehow excess is built in.

Under new management, Columbia Pictures celebrated its fiftieth anniversary in 1974 where it had begun—at absolute zero. The money Columbia lost in 1958–59, 1961, and 1970–72 added up to $87 million, which is exactly the amount it had made in all the profitable years since the brothers Jack and Harry Cohn founded the company in 1924.

To replace Jaffe and pull the company back from the sea of red ink, Columbia chose former superagent and cofounder of Creative Management Associates (CMA) David Begelman. In his first news conference, Begelman said his first priority would be to bring Columbia into the mainstream, by which he was referring to a neat way of embracing the *auteur* theory that made directors all-important. He planned to make one-film deals with directors such as Martin Ritt (*Sounder*), George Roy Hill (*The Sting*), John Boorman (*Deliverance*), Francis Ford Coppola (*Godfather I* and *II*), and Franklin Schaffner (*Papillon*), while cleaning out executives and big-time producers and hiring AIP's "new math" whiz kid Lawrence A. Gordon, whose specialty was getting high-priced writers cheap by giving them their first opportunity to direct. "I feel that in the past several years Columbia has been a strongly producer-oriented company and I think there should be a short line between the people making the decisions at Columbia and the people who actually make the films—a shorter, leaner line."

Begelman demanded trims. Producers were told to slash budgets by script rewrites and were asked to accept reduced fees and lower percentages of eventual profits. "Each picture to us represents a substantial investment, and any picture we have we're going to treat as though it's the only one," Begelman said, inaugurating what he called a rolled-up-sleeves approach. The Begelman regime's first slate was, predictably, a mixed bag, ranging from Robert Altman's *California Split*, Joseph Mankiewicz's *Jane*, and Steven Spielberg's *Close Encounter of the Third Kind* to such items as *Funny Lady* (the laundered continuation of *Funny Girl*), *The Onion Field*, and another Charles Bronson starrer, *The Ten-Second Jail Break*, plus Ken Russell's first-in-America, *Karate Is a Thing of the Spirit*.

"Television has fallen into a format which is limiting," Begelman said a year after taking office. "It doesn't give the sense of fulfill-ment motion pictures do. By its nature, television has too many strictures, and the happiest situation is that there are no restrictions in motion pictures."

Also in 1973, United Artists—the only major still headquartered in Manhattan, although taking orders from San Francisco—changed leadership. Austrian-born Eric Pleskow was named presi-dent, taking over from David Picker, a young and wealthy second-generation theaterman who had surrounded himself with aggres-sive, no-nonsense, but hip people. Picker, who was not pushed out in a sea of red ink but left to become an independent gentleman-producer releasing through UA, didn't always take himself too seriously. He once suggested that if in any one year UA did every project it had turned down and said no to every project it eventu-ally did bring to the screen, the result might be the same number of hits and flops.

"Today we're ruled by cost accountants," said Pleskow when he took over. The main influence of Transamerica Corporation on UA (and of Gulf & Western president Charles Bluhdorn on Paramount) has been in bookkeeping, which, until the corporate takeovers, was unorthodox, to say the least. Pleskow, who has been with UA since 1951 and has been stationed in South Africa and Germany, feels directors and talent must agree to share costs, risks, and potential profits.

"We're always thinking hard," says Pleskow. "I don't want to lock myself in and knock myself out of competition. We spend the kind of money it takes to put together an intelligent, forceful pro-gram that we think makes economic sense."

Companies still itch to get into the glamour business. UA had Reader's Digest as a partner in *Tom Sawyer*, but made its recent "killing" with *The Last Tango in Paris*.

Like MGM's Rosenfelt, Twentieth Century–Fox's Gordon Stul-berg is a former lawyer. When Stulberg drives through the West Los Angeles studio gates the first thing he sees is the $2 million set of *Hello, Dolly!* the extravaganza on which Fox lost a staggering $16 million.

"That set is a monument to man's stupidity," says Manny Gerard, a partner of Roth Gerard & Company, an analyst of the entertainment industry. "If I were running Fox I'd never tear it down. I'd want to keep it there as a reminder of the grim past."

Stulberg wasn't around when Fox made *Dolly*. And he has no plans to tear down the elevated railroad, the church front, the bank, and other plywood evidence of the major flop. But the set is about the only reminder of the Darryl Zanuck management that Stulberg has left untouched. In his and chairman (and fellow lawyer) Dennis Stanfill's tenure at Fox they have fired hundreds of employes, instituted drastic cost-cutting policies, and, with *The Poseidon Adventure*, started a fiscal turnaround. They paid off $100,000 in loans, renegotiated debt, secured a $44 million line of new credit, and for 1973 managed to make a profit of $7.6 million.

Before joining Fox, Stulberg was the president of CBS's short-lived Cinema Center Films, losing $20 million in two years. Stulberg says the Center had such large losses largely because of a CBS accounting practice. CCF, he contends, was charged interest by its parent company on money CBS advanced for film production.

Stulberg, whose annual Fox salary is $200,000 plus bonuses, says that he shies away from films containing social commentaries because what the public is interested in when a picture is written may no longer be a boxoffice attraction when it has been completed.

"I look for entertainment in the broadest sense," says Stulberg. "I want the picture to be broad enough to attract everyone. I want our movies to appeal equally to the steel mill operator in Erie, Pennsylvania, and to the college girl in New York City."

What caused the downfall of the Zanuck regime?

"Bad dealmaking," Stulberg told *The Los Angeles Times* shortly after his appointment.[5] "By bad dealmaking I mean making up your mind to produce a film at any cost. It means the business affair people have no strength."

Stulberg doesn't believe in "event pictures" such as *The Godfather* and *The Exorcist*, because they were what led to "the *Sound of Music–Hello, Dolly!* syndrome, which sent everyone searching after event pictures no matter what cost," and he refuses to outbid others for "hot" scripts. Fox was first offered Joseph Wambaugh's first best seller, *The New Centurions*, but turned it down because the $500,000 price tag was deemed too high. As directed by Richard Fleischer for Columbia, *The New Centurions* became a modest success, earning $7.5 million during its first year of release.

Under Gulf & Western president Charles Bluhdorn's back-seat

5. *Los Angeles Times*, Nov. 14, 1971.

control, Paramount Pictures is run by Barry Diller, a former television wunderkind who more or less invented the Movie-of-the Week concept for ABC-TV. Born in 1942, Diller is the youngest of the contemporary moguls. He took over from Frank Yablans, an outspoken but square executive who hates critics and film festivals, after Yablans' superhype for *The Great Gatsby* misfired.

Yablans shared Paramount's greatest glory, *The Godfather*, with Robert Evans, a reformed clothing manufacturer and failed actor who ruled the studio for seven years. Still senior vice-president in charge of production, Evans has also become an independent producer for Paramount—a position that allows him to get a piece of the action of the pictures he pushes. As executive vice-president he was not cut in on the financial windfalls of such hat tricks of his as *Love Story* and *The Godfather*.

In the middle of his tenure, Yablans said his salary was not for being instinctively right, but professionally right. He felt the 1960s were the decade when the industry grew up and studios began to be incorporated into business structures. The blackest period, he says, was the early 1950s. The retirement or death of the Samuel Goldwyns, Louis B. Mayers, and Harry Cohns who ruled their lots like caliphs, buying stars like steers and firing directors as easily as office boys, was traumatic for Hollywood. The studios had been one-man or one-family operations, and the successors were unable to carry over the style of the founding fathers.

"Word-of-mouth continues to be the largest single factor in the success of a film," says Yablans. "There is no greater selling point than to have an audience come out of a film saying they liked it. Films are still a very young business and despite all the roadblocks that have been set in their path, they have managed not only to survive but to prosper despite what at times have been tremendous odds."

In the 1970s Warner's is as vigorous and imaginative as when James Cagney, Bette Davis, Humphrey Bogart, and black-and-white populist melodrama made it the grittiest of the dream factories. When Jack Warner sold out in 1967 he was the last (and youngest) of the founding fathers to call it quits, and after the two-year hitch with Seven Arts Productions, the company became a subsidiary of Kinney National. Its boss was Ted Ashley, until 1969 best known as the former head of Ashley Famous Talent Agency.

Ashley, who rarely gives interviews, started his career as a sixteen-year-old office boy in the William Morris Agency and was a full-fledged agent by the time he was twenty. Under his leadership, Warner's has tried to sail on an even keel. It began its youth orientation with *Woodstock*, but, wisely perhaps, hasn't tried to pinpoint films for any special fragment of the filmgoing public. Its range has spanned the spectrum from *A Clockwork Orange* and *Deliverance* to *Superfly*, *Klute*, and *Dirty Harry*, and in so doing its gross income rose from $77 million in 1971 to $145 million in 1973. With *The Exorcist* and, to a degree, *Magnum Force*, the bloody, brutal sequel to *Dirty Harry*, Warner's first quarter in 1974 reached an all-time high of $16 million in profits.

On January 1, 1975, John Calley took over from the retiring Ashley, becoming president while retaining his post as executive vice-president in charge of production. Calley's professional style is one of selective interest and pursuit of favored projects (with *A Clockwork Orange*, he brought Stanley Kubrick to Warner's). He is a producer who swears by the youth market. "That doesn't mean you have to make youth films," says Calley, who, like his former boss, Ashley, sports a full beard. "By the time a kid is eighteen he's assimilated so much visual information he's developed a critical sense. Plot doesn't seem to do it—you can see plots by the hour on television. Good characterization and a sense of reality help a lot. The director's problem is imparting reality and encouraging good characterization. Film, by its definition, must be different."

Calley's work habits and manner are casual. He does not wear a tie at the office and does not use a desk. Instead there is a large table cluttered with memos, art books, and manuscripts, and in the middle of it a statue of a little man looking at a stock-market tape. Around the table are comfortable sofas, and visitors are invited to plunk their feet on the table.

"If there's a trend, it's less a budgetary thing than it is the emergence of the director as the prime force," says Calley. Television is now the manufacturing process that the studios once were. The producer-as-powerhouse has generally been replaced by the director and, in some instances, by the collaboration of the writer and director."

The Disney organization is an inexhaustible gold mine. Its 1973 profits were $47 million, with over 60 percent of the revenues coming from amusement parks. Admired by Albert Einstein and loved by millions, the world of Walt Disney has prevailed. "The financial fellows think we're going to fall on our faces without Walt," said his brother Roy O. Disney a few months after Walt's death in 1966. Eight years later, Walt Disney Productions was the only blue-chip stock in show business. The company remains essentially a tightly knit family affair. The heirs of Walt and Roy O. (who died in 1971) retain the largest single block of the stock. President E. Cardon Walker, fifty-seven, and Chairman Donn B. Tatum, sixty, both joined the Disney brothers in the thirties; executive producer Ronald W. Miller is Walt's son-in-law, and Roy Disney's son, Roy E. Disney, heads TV projects.

A quiet revolution has taken place inside the terra cotta studio built in the first flush of *Snow White*'s astounding success in 1937. "We're getting liberated—like everybody else," says Wolfgang ("Woolie") Reitherman, the director of all Disney animated features and, as such, head man on artistic direction in the sphere where it all started—cartooning. "The last word here is to let the story tell itself. We try to tell the story more through situations and character than through plot and story line." For forty years, Walt Disney Productions have lived by one law—"full animation." Characters are drawn with care and their actions made smooth through hundreds of thousands of separate sketches (a full-length Disney cartoon is made up of about 300,000 separate drawings). If Mickey Mouse, Bambi, Pluto, or the new Robin Hood have to throw a ball, the gesture is drawn in sufficient detail to be smooth and graceful. The same gesture in a TV cartoon or avant-garde short will be accomplished in a few jerky drawings. Although this "minimal animation" may be valid and have its charm in the short cartoon, it is usually unacceptable in full-length features. "To capture and hold very young persons' attention for an hour and a half, you've got to have more than pretty drawings and abstract gestures," says Reitherman. "The liberation of Mickey Mouse is in the story concept, in the choice of voices and talents."

American International Pictures (AIP), the major of the minors, is run by chain-smoking Samuel Z. Arkoff. "For years people in the business would say, 'Oh, them, they make exploitation films.' They kept right on saying that until word got around that AIP and Disney were the only consistently profitable operations in town," relates Arkoff with a grin.

A company with a building on Beverly Hills's Wilshire Boulevard, offices in New York and London, three hundred employes, and a listing on the American Stock Exchange, AIP is still "the king of the B's."

"So far we've been lucky," says Arkoff, a candid and witty man given to introspection. "We've guessed what the audience wanted. Too many moviemakers make their pictures for their peers, for the Beverly Hills circuit. We use name stars even less than most studios. We always have, now it's that way nearly everywhere. With a few exceptions, stars don't make films. It's the other way around—films make stars. Look at Peter Fonda, Dennis Hopper, and Jack Nicholson. We used them first and our films did a lot for them."

AIP has made a fortune by being tuned to the very young ("we have a rule: no parents, or church or school authorities, in our films"), with the interminable list of beach blanket bikini movies, some admirable horror flicks, *Wild in the Streets* protest quickies, bike pictures, and shrewd neoromantic froth (its remake of *Wuthering Heights*, however, was a bomb).

Arkoff formed AIP together with the late James Nicholson in 1954, the year RKO and Republic Pictures International went under and most of the majors were tightening their belts. Their first picture, *Apache Woman*, was a Republic-style shoot 'em up, and it took eight years to break even. By the time AIP squeaked into the black, however, Arkoff and Nicholson were rich men gladly suffering the disdain of Hollywood, for they had made a fortune turning out minibudget movies in three weeks, two at a time, filling drive-in double bills and their bank account. By 1959, the low-budget double bills ("combinations," in AIP vernacular) appeared headed downhill, and Arkoff and Nicholson decided to up the budgets, switching to color and a wide screen. Their $3.5 million gamble was *The House of Usher*, starring Vincent Price and directed by Roger Corman, AIP's "house director" for over ten years. It worked, and AIP is still churning out Edgar Allan Poe horrors.

"We haven't made a drug picture since *The Trip* with Peter Fonda," says Arkoff. "That was before *Easy Rider*. Look at all the dope pictures that came after that: all of them failures. You fly by the seat of your pants in this business. So far we've been lucky. We've guessed what the audience wanted. We think first of the audience and I feel that's why all of our youth-oriented pictures have succeeded. The secret, I think, is eternal pertinent issues."

Easy Rider, which cost $400,000 and grossed $25 million, almost became an AIP effort. The Columbia gold mine was not a happy accident; its players, characters, terrain, and story had been market-tested and its crew developed over half a dozen AIP pictures. *The Wild Angels*, with Fonda as the leader of an outlaw motorcycle gang, had cost $350,000 and grossed AIP $5 million, making it "the biggest grossing low-budget picture made at that time," according to director Corman. A close second was *The Trip*, also directed by Corman, this time with Fonda as a TV director on a drug trip. He was supported by Hopper in a script written by Nicholson. Both Hopper and Nicholson had appeared individually in previous bike pictures, Hopper in *The Glory Stompers* and Nicholson as a poet in *Hell's Angels on Wheels*. In *Psych-out* Nicholson had explored the hippie scene. When Fonda conceived and put together *Easy Rider* and presented it to Arkoff, AIP had reservations about Hopper directing it. Since it was Hopper's first film as a director, Arkoff wanted a contract provision allowing him to replace Hopper if he went over the budget. Instead, Fonda walked over to Columbia, where producer Burt Schneider looked at the proposed budget and the track record of the previous AIP bike movies. "The rest," *Variety* commented, "is film history." [6]

That AIP hasn't lost its touch is proved by the constant raiding of its sideburned young "gun slinger" executives by other studios. Begelman had barely taken over Columbia when he lured low-budget whiz kid Lawrence A. Gordon away from Arkoff, installing the former ABC-TV packager as head of an independent company furnishing films exclusively for Columbia. As AIP's production vice-president, Gordon paid particular attention to script development, gave lots of graduating film students their first chances, and invented the black-audience-oriented movie—inevitably called the "blaxploitation" film after such AIP items as *Blacula*, *Slaughter*, and *Coffey*. Before he left, he put together *Sugar Hill*, the story of a black lady taking revenge on mobster characters with the help of voodoo and occult sciences.

Throughout its history, the film industry has lived a Greek tragedy—financial *hubris* leading swiftly and blindly to disaster before a phoenix-like ascension from its own ashes. Even if Leo the Lion seems to be near his last roar—despite Rosenfelt's reassurances to the contrary, it is simply not realistic to finance a roster of films without controlling their distribution—most of the original companies of this hotheaded and extravagant industry are still here. In 1924 there were fourteen daily newspapers in New York City; by 1967, inflation, stubborn unions, internecine wars, and television had reduced them to three. The 1924 line-up of movie companies included Columbia, Disney, First National, Monogram, MGM, RKO, Fox, Paramount, United Artists, Universal, and Warner Brothers. Although their founders or their descendants are no longer in control, all but First National, Monogram, RKO, and now MGM are still at it.

3

The View from Left Field

THE WORKS of some of America's most talented filmmakers never see the inside of *any* studio. Robert Altman may make *M*A*S*H* for Fox, *McCabe and Mrs. Miller* for Warner's, *Thieves Like Us* for UA, and *California Split* for Columbia without ever moving himself and his menagerie of stock players and collaborators onto or off any lot. George Lucas may do *American Graffiti* with Universal's money and *Star Wars* with Fox's bankroll, but his center of gravity remains Mill Valley on the north shore of San Francisco Bay. Stanley Kubrick makes movies for Warner's, but for the past decade he has lived in England.

Altman, Lucas, and Kubrick are, together with a handful of others, the straws in the wind, as Claude Monet and the Impressionists were the beginning of modern art because with them the significance shifted from subject to the artist's own *presence* on the canvas. Altman's and Kubrick's films may never cease to tell a story, but, like Manet painting the youthful Georges Clemenceau, *they* are becoming everything in the portrait and Clemenceau next to nothing. Delacroix's Chopin and Ingres's Bertin are portraits in the grand manner, belonging not to the artist but to the model. Madame Charpentier, as André Malraux has said, is no longer a portrait of a lady of society, it is a Renoir.

What films have to say and how they say it have changed. A combination of factors—shifting tastes, the general fracturing of the arts, and new economic realities—are the causes of change. Zoomin shots and rock music applied like body paint on the sound track are the effects.

What is new with the screen's best artists is a deeper understanding of the subterranean wealth of the medium. Modern cinema has absorbed what preceded it: the narrative experiments of the last decade, the devices of time and structure. Modern films try to explore themselves.

Tentatively, a "modern film" can be defined as follows:

● It moves. It isn't "photographed theater," as Alfred Hitchcock once said, but advances organically. It is storytelling freed of discursive style and with a forward thrust that is less logical than obsessive; storytelling that doesn't stress plot and character, but emotional contradictions and ambiguity.

● It is honest—a much-abused word, here meaning that the movie doesn't talk *down* to its audience, doesn't try to con or to pander. Honesty also means letting contradictions happen, letting scenes "breathe," be loose enough to let reality impose changes.

● It is relevant; it "has something to say" and is meaningful beyond mere consumerism.

● It explores itself; sees things differently, as inner patterns and designs, and nips its audience in surprising ways.

"I tell the story and extract its meaning," says John Boorman, "by taking into account rhythm, pace, structure, the story's architecture, its emotional forces."

Although appealing to different senses, modern movies, like modern novels, are often slim volumes. The new cinema likes metaphor and hyperbole. There is often a certain offhandedness, a distance, a "cool," even in committed works. Emotions are not necessarily achieved through detail, but may come across through staging, the story's angle of attack, its point of view.

Instead of a series of carefully examined circumstances that add up to a social and psychological portrait or dramatized "life," a story is often pulled together in a crisis which itself is the result of haphazard events but becomes crucial to one or more characters. Chance happenings give urgency and allow fleeting setups. The past is evoked in rapid flashbacks, and instead of following a story episode by episode, we are confronted with a suspended present, an ephemeral yet significant now in which everything is reflected and distilled. This "amplified now" makes pitch and tone all important. Characters must impose on us as individuals who are *present*, while we watch them not just as people whose story we are being told. The filmmaker is not a puppeteer, pulling character strings and railroading audience responses. Players are often chosen for their ability to think on the screen, to portray a character thinking rather than a character acting. Typically, intense new directors often cannot make up their minds whether to document their obsessions or to fictionalize them.

Directors of a more innocent age were making pictures and having a good time. They made up their own rules—and broke them—as they went along, and were only by accident artists. "The big problem for a director today is to get back to that spirit of innocence, directness, and simplicity," Peter Bogdanovich has said. But the relationship between director and his material has changed *in terms of film*. New filmmaking means going beyond the subject. The director often appears only as a monitor of records, and his "art" is limited to his choice of scenes and their juxtaposition. When he becomes "personal," he may only express his feelings in the film's form, not its content. For the screen's top artists, plot is often mere pretext.

Since the fade-in in 1872 when a bearded codger with the flavorful name of Eadwaerd Muybridge produced the first sequence of moving pictures, the movies have evolved in often baffling directions. Born of dime-store literature and vaudeville, the cinema grew up comfortably middlebrow and only mutated under stress.

With moviegoing no longer habit-forming in affluent societies, American movies are nevertheless the chief purveyor of sight and sound communications across the borders. The main difference between American and other national cinemas is still that the world—with obvious political exceptions—sees nearly all American films, but only the proverbial iceberg's tip of Italian, Japanese, and Argentinian productions. Most of the world's screenfare is made for home consumption; American movies are the exception.

To have one's name under the *directed by* line on the credit crawl is said to be the closest anyone can come to Divine Power. Film directors have been likened to field generals and analysts, but better than Napoleon and Freud, they can—like gods—distort facts, freeze time, reshape history and, traditionally, make actors and audiences think and feel along preestablished lines.

The director is a person through whose emotions the film is brought to the screen; a person—rarely seen—who is in control of story, set, cast, pace, and mood. Diplomat, nursemaid, bully, seducer, and often boom-voiced autocrat, today's top director is more often than not the film's prime mover, with control from concept to delivery of the final work. Significantly, the more encompassing title of filmmaker—with or without hyphen—is increasingly used.

A director riding a success wave can command half a million dollars per picture plus percentages and virtually unlimited creative control. He belongs to the elite, is protected by the powerful Directors' Guild of America, is feted and flattered in the best circles, and is the object of cults. This is heady wine for many who often spent years scratching, hacking, and begging to get the chance to work as they please.

The (re)discovery of the director began in the late 1950s, although the real impetus, both in America and Europe, didn't start until 1960. Critics received a thunderbolt at the 1951 Venice Film Festival when they saw Akira Kurosawa's *Rashomon*. In technique, the film was traumatically original. This medieval tale of a bandit, a nobleman, his wife, and an involuntary witness of a crime was a study of ambiguities, but it was big and strong. Kurosawa, who was forty-one when the picture was shown in Venice, was originally a painter. He made moviegoers sit up and take notice. The next revelation was Ingmar Bergman.

Critical awareness of the filmmaker antedates the 1951 Venice festival, of course. The 1920s saw the first serious writings on film, notably in the budding Soviet cinema and in fervent bohemias in Berlin and Paris. In the early 1930s, Louis Delluc, Germaine Dullac, and Marcel L'Herbier founded the rich French school of film scholarship, leading to André Bazin, the founder in 1951 of *Cahiers du Cinéma*, a canary-colored monthly magazine whose influence extended far beyond its comparatively modest circulation. *Cahiers* set the world of film criticism on its ears, recruiting disciples and compelling opponents to think again, only to flounder in far-out Maoist dialectics after the May 1968 student uprising that radicalized most French intellectuals.

It was in the January 1954 issue of *Cahiers* that François Truffaut wrote an essay which somehow stands at the beginning of the *politique des auteurs*, a term Andrew Sarris translated as the *auteur* theory (leaving the key word in French to avoid the literary connotation of "author" in English). Attacking well-upholstered, well-acted, carefully motivated French "quality" filmmaking and its verbal tyranny, Truffaut listed Jean Renoir, Max Ophuls, Robert Bresson, and Jacques Tati as authentic *auteurs*. The *Cahiers* line reflected an attitude more than a manifesto or collective statement, but it came as a shock to English-speaking movie buffs and filmmakers that the gods of the New Wave Frenchmen were Hollywood veterans. And not Orson Welles and Charles Chaplin with their grand humanistic themes, but makers of snappy B pictures that didn't get bogged down with lofty messages, and of action westerns that knew how to shoot straight. Whereas British and American critics tended to grade movies according to their social values, the fiery Parisians with their pleasingly romantic view of America tried to look beyond content to form, beyond performance to pattern and structure.

Too much attention was being paid to humanist themes, they claimed, to the way things are said, and not enough to the way things are staged, their style, their *mise en scène*—that virtually untranslatable Gallicism meaning as much elucidation and creation of mood and ambiance as, literally, directing actors from camera-left to camera-right and visualizing a text in three dimensions. A routine western could be a piece of pure *mise en scène*. We know the bad guy will be killed, but *how* is this staged? Is the camera saying it? Are we allowed to "read" more from the screen than its surface significance? A dolly shot tracking him along a wall to the fatal stumbling can be a "privileged moment" because it is cinematic in its essence.

Owing to the erosion of the original theory, the *auteur* credo today means practically anything that somehow enhances the director's prestige. Yet it is essentially a backward glance, an after-the-fact, *a posteriori* examination of a filmmaker's work. If one could see *all* of Howard Hawks's films at one time, or all of John Ford's, themes would come into focus. Both made westerns, but Hawks's westerns exalt a kind of male "elite," whereas Ford's heroes always *belong*, are individuals within society. For Hawks, men are equals and must strive to retain their mastery. In Ford's films, women are not a threat. Heroes in Hawks's pictures pride themselves on their professionalism. "When they die, they leave behind them only the most meager personal belongings, perhaps a handful of medals," Peter Wollen has written in a comparative analysis. "In Ford films, death is celebrated by funeral services, an impromptu prayer, a few staves of 'Shall we gather at the river?'—it is inserted into an ongoing system of ritual institutions, along with the wedding, the dance, the parade. But for Hawks it is enough that the routine of the group's life goes on, a routine whose only relieving features are 'danger' (*Hatari!*) and 'fun' " [1]

The renewed film scholarship of the fifties also led to a reexamination of the cinematic language. The *Cahiers* crowd often came closer to understanding how movies worked than many professionals. When Truffaut, Jean-Luc Godard, Claude Chabrol, Jacques Doniol-Valcroze, and Eric Rohmer spent their own money, or their wives' and parents', and borrowed equipment from each other to make their first features, they tried to apply their theories—to show thinking in movement, to detach characters by giving them recitative speech, and to bring across inner duration, so different from dramatic time. In *Un Couple* (1962) Jean-Pierre Mocky had a piece of modern *mise en scène* of exemplary simplicity: a man and a woman undressing amorously in front of each other. Whereas such sequences are usually staged in such a manner as to give the audience a chance to enjoy the girl's striptease, Mocky had her undress "in the story," so to speak, for the benefit of her companion, not for the camera.

Alain Resnais refused traditional exposition-crisis-resolution storytelling and instead tried narrations in "decrescendo," going from crisis to separation to despair. Others experimented with *temps faibles*, those undramatic weak moments when nothing happens. A classic example is Robert Bresson's 1950 adaptation of Georges Bernanos' *Le Journal d'un Curé de Campagne*. Bresson had his country priest open and close innumerable doors and gates throughout the picture. The total effect was a filmic equivalent of the claustrophobia that made Bernanos' novel so haunting. There was even a feedback of cinematic storytelling to the new novel. Alain Robbe-Grillet, Michel Butor, and Pierre Gascar adapted such filmic devices as "inner discourse" or offscreen narration, flashbacks, and condensation and compression of duration into a "now." They wrote in fragmentary style, in which progression was less a matter of narrative logic than of obsessive thrusts, as in a Michelangelo Antonioni film. "One of Antonioni's greater merits is that he has

1. Peter Wollen, *Sights and Meaning in the Cinema*. Bloomington: Indiana University Press, 1969.

caught in a net of refined dramaturgy all the *lost meanings* that make up our everyday lives," wrote Christian Metz.[2]

Meanwhile, theorists came up with other findings, such as the projection-identification process. Audiences, they discovered, are not primarily attracted to the opposite sex on the screen, but project themselves on the light-and-shadow figures of their own sex. Male spectators project themselves on, say, Sean Connery and live James Bond fantasies *through* him, and women identify with Jane Fonda or Joanne Woodward. Gilbert Cohen-Séat wrote that movies' special suggestivity created an emotional state that, instead of heightening the mental level, enslaved audiences in a series of psychological "tensions and miseries."

And how can this degrading effect be overcome?, the theorists asked. Jean Carta postulated that "a movie is humanistic insofar as it does not enslave its audience, but, on the contrary, gives its spectators a chance to free themselves from its spell so as to judge it." [3] Sergei Eisenstein, who sought the elusive unity of science and art and made what is still considered the most daring silent movie, *Potemkin*, when he was twenty-six, was found to be the villain. Eisenstein saw in the movies a supreme tool of thought-control because the filmmaker can make his audience feel and react as he pleases. Adding the voyeur impulse to the director's arsenal of manipulative powers, Alfred Hitchcock was also seen as a master of cinematic straightjacketing.

The search for a way to make movies that would permit lucid viewing rather than spellbinding fascination led to the discovery that instances of perfect humanism could be found, of all places, in Hollywood pictures of the 1940s. Both Orson Welles and William Wyler had forced audiences to *judge* between simultaneous actions. With deep-focus lenses, they managed to stage simultaneous actions in foregrounds and backgrounds of the same shot. By making these actions conflict, the directors forced their audiences to apply critical judgment to the screen.

A next step was cinéma-vérité, a form of moviemaking made possible through technical innovations and perfections in film stock, camera construction, and magnetic tape recordings. Invented by New York and Montreal documentarians, cinéma-vérité was enthu-

2. Christian Metz, *"Le Cinéma Moderne et la Narrativité," Cahiers du Cinéma*, Dec. 1966.

3. Jean Carta, *Esprit*, June 1960.

siastically adopted by new directors working in from the fringe and by filmmakers in "emerging countries," trying to go beyond consumer esthetics toward a cinema that could mirror political and moral issues. Together with the maturing French New Wave, this "new cinema" showed it could give its audiences "a certain kind of truth (*vérité*), rarely found in the better films of the past," as Metz said, "truths that are infinitely difficult to define, but that we recognize almost instinctively—gestures, tones, inflections that are right on target."

In the United States, the forward thrust also came from the fringe—makers of TV commercials regularly ransack avant-garde films for ideas—but American newcomers had different sources of inspiration. Scratch a European filmmaker, it was said, and you will find a former critic or a would-be writer. Scratch an American undergrounder and you will find a former painter or sculptor. At their best, American experimental films were passionate attempts at New Things leading to "expanded cinema" and "mixed media environments," in which movies, theater, recorded music, kinetic sculpture, and light painting were fused into a single engulfing experience. Compared with this "parallel" moviemaking, Hollywood's output of a "safe," almost ritual cinema, based on time-honored values of best-seller source material, star-studded casts, and "production values," increasingly looked cumbersome and obsolete. But the no-longer-underground esthetic was seeping into the visual vocabulary, and by 1970 a "Hollywood movie" was often as snazzy as a Lower Manhattan radical's short.

Irony is rarely absent from human affairs, and it is indeed ironic that the ascent of the director should come at a time when, in Western art, the assumption that a great work is the creation of a single mind is being challenged. Even more ironic is the fact that the new freedom has come at a moment when, literally, the cinema can least afford it.

American directors are as varied as the movies they make, and if the History of Motion Pictures is notably short of geniuses, it nevertheless contains a fair sprinkling of headstrong men and even a few tragic figures. Despite the herd instinct that is so apparent in the choice of story material, there is no reason to believe new filmmakers will turn out to be less individualistic than their elders.

But a "young" and "new" filmmaker can mean many things:

- The nineteen-year-old UCLA freshman making a twenty-minute agitprop documentary on ghetto injustice.
- The twenty-nine-year-old newcomer preparing his second feature for Paramount.
- The thirty-nine-year-old producer-director of Warner's current smash hit grossing $36,000 in the second week at Manhattan's Cinema II (after opening-week earnings of $28,000).
- The forty-nine-year-old *auteur* of the season's surprise "sleeper," called a "must" by *Esquire* and *The Village Voice*.

Youth is in the eyes of the beholder, and not in the kneecaps of the guy yelling "Action!" and "Cut!"

Traditionally, the movies were never part of the Young Man's Burden. True, Orson Welles was twenty-six when he made *Citizen Kane*, and Sergei Eisenstein twenty-seven when he finished *Potemkin*, but they were exceptions in the *wunderkind* tradition of showbiz legends. If anything, filmmaking is a crap game for maturer men with a sharp eye for spotting new trends, or, perhaps even more important, a nose fine enough to smell when a trend is over. Cinematic relevance is a matter of staying power.

The significant films of the 1969–70 "youthquake," for example, were made by directors in their thirties, forties, and even fifties. The year Altman hit the Big Time after a long and frustrating apprenticeship, he also became a grandfather. Melvin Van Peebles was thirty-eight when he hit with *Sweet Sweetback's Badaaasss Song*; Sam Peckinpah was forty-two when he made *The Wild Bunch*, and Arthur Penn forty-eight when *Little Big Man* reached the screen.

A director's feat is to square the circle: to make films striking enough to draw the audience but not so alienating as to drive it away. His forward thrust is on the thin line between the jaded and the too-far-out. He must avoid the threadbare as well as the "artsy-craftsy." Sometimes a "winner" displays its novelty in subject matter rather than artistic development; sometimes it's all form.

There is no such thing as "pure cinema," regardless of the political climate a filmmaker works in. If anything, "progressive" countries are less than tolerant of art for art's sake. Nowhere are filmmakers given funds to make flop after flop—that is, films too far ahead or too far above what *any* audience will tolerate. Such artistic aloofness is possible only in less expensive arts. Cézanne and Van Gogh were barely cold in their graves before art dealers descended on their works, but during their lives they never sold a canvas. Such righteous stubbornness and ultimate, if posthumous, vindication is unthinkable in the movies. Cinema is perhaps the only art where creative people also have to worry about being businessmen.

Unless a filmmaker respects the needs of an audience, he cannot complain that audiences fail to show up. Boring in from the fringe, newcomers are naturally insecure and likely to join rhetorical fraternities and talk about a new "noncommercial" cinema. But even *they* want an audience, enough patrons to recoup their investment so as to plunge into another film. Fortunately, the merging of the commercial film with the art film seems again more than likely, as audiences' expectations are heightened and filmmakers leave the more strident "revolutionary" rhetoric behind them.

Despite the arduous reshaping of forms and ideas, such hothouse societies as Jonas Mekas' Film-Makers Cooperative—a nonprofit rental library on New York's Lexington Avenue which over the years has become the haven for vanguard, offbeat, experimental and underground cinema—remain way stations toward some kind of Big Time. Most newcomers display a healthy appetite for commercial success and, after a first major feature, an illuminating respect for "pro moviemaking." They no longer feel they have to perform public apostasy if their movies also happen to make money.

With the possible exception of French-Canadian *cinéastes*, success in North America inevitably leads to Hollywood—that is, to a professional attitude toward film and work. Extended amateurism somehow is not in the American grain.

Also, despite the perennial talk of "outside financing" and the creation of a "parallel cinema," more goodwill than hard cash is raised in this manner. Syndicates of investors are nothing new, but such financial backers often have unrealistic notions of what movies are, and most filmmakers prefer to abandon this form of money raising as soon as they have enough muscle or a sufficiently exciting project to command attention from a major. Outside money tends to be nervous, unreliable, and costly, and to sour very easily.

As Shirley Clarke said, "Anyone trying hard enough can make a first film; it's the second that counts." Recent history is littered with so many "first features," put together with enthusiasm, good luck, deferred payments, and unconquerable faith, that newcomers talk about the "one-shot-director barrier," as John Avildsen called it after his *Joe* success. An appalling number of first works never make

it to *any* market.[4] A small fraction do triumph over multiple vicissi-
tudes, but their makers, hailed as fresh and promising new talents,
are either never heard from again or, more frequently, nosedive
into oblivion after a second time out. A partial list of recent young
filmmakers never heard from again includes Hollywoodites like
James Frawley (the maker of the never-released *Christian Licorice
Store* and the Dennis Hopper starrer *Kid Blue*), Bob Rafaelson (*Five
Easy Pieces* and *The King of Marvin Gardens*), Henry Jaglom (*A Safe
Place*), and writers trying their luck such as Floyd Mutrux (*Dusty
and Sweet McGee*) and Charles Eastman (*The All-American Boy* with
Jon Voight). Age of Aquarius celebrities who disappeared include
Stuart Hagman (the maker of MGM's 1970 campus revolt opus *The
Strawberry Statement* and the drug-themed *Believe in Me*), Paul Wil-
liams (*The Revolutionary*, also with Voight), and *Woodstock*'s own
Michael Wadleigh. New Yorkers in and out of film are Seymour
Robbie (*C. C. and Company*, with Joe Namath and Ann-Margret),
Milton Ginsberg (*Coming Apart*), Bill Norton (*Cisco Pike*), Paul
Sylbert (*The Steagle*), and Stan Dragoti (*Dirty Little Billy*), while
overseas Americans include Susan Sontag (*Broder Carl* in Sweden),
Robert Kramer (*Ice* in France), and Conrad Rooks (*Siddhartha* in
India).

What happened? Their first or second picture was not a success
at the boxoffice. "New York is the most fantastic film showcase in
the world; it's also the toughest place for a movie to survive," says
cameraman-turned-director-turned-cameraman-again Michael Nebbia. "If a film isn't an immediate smash hit, it craps out in its initial
engagement and the distributor often loses his interest. The
numbers can be devastating for an offbeat film that, at best, can an-
ticipate a mixed press." Nebbia's *Life Study* was shown at the First
Avenue Screening Room, a mid-Manhattan theater which has become a rescue operation for some of these casualties.

"Young people confuse the romanticism concerned with motion
pictures with the *business* of motion pictures," says Hollywood veteran King Vidor. "The difference in making pictures yesterday and
today is that Metro's almighty Irving Thalberg could take chances
because he knew that under the booking system he was guaranteed
an audience for any film. Of course, he might get a much larger au-

---

4. The phenomenon is by no means exclusively an American aberration. In 1972 *L'Express*
established that between 1968 and 1971 thirty-seven full-length features by new directors
failed to get *any* distribution in France.

dience for a successful picture, but the audience was there for *any* film. Today this is simply not true. Any talk about movies makes no sense unless one faces the fact that the automatic audience has vanished and that a picture must make it on its own."

Radical circles like to blame "the system" and to call Columbia, Fox, *et al.* the archvillains conspiring to keep out young and true talent. The very word "industry" is dirty. In reality, the majors have gone to considerable lengths—and in the process lost hefty sums—to attract and bankroll what seemed to be tomorrow's wave.

Big, almost ritualistic movies, which try to have it every which way, and whose subjects are chosen for their power to produce responses rather than for their appeal, fail as cheerfully at the box-office as "new films," and usually with more disastrous results, since these mechanical biggies, with their time-honored "values" of best-seller source material and starry casts, cost so much more than the newcomers' tentative pictures. Yet cutting budgets has not seemed to be the answer to audience defection.

Shocking examples of mishandling of independent films by the majors still abound, and the present generation of studio bosses sometimes seems no more enlightened than its monarchic forefathers. Yet, on the other side, film-festival attempts to "rescue" movies supposedly trampled over by callous majors rarely have any discernible results.

"You're as good as your last picture," goes the old Hollywood adage, sometimes expressed negatively as "Nobody's better than his last picture." A movie's appeal translates into "body counts," whether these are expressed in numbers of admissions or in boxoffice yen, pounds, rubles, or dollars. The maddening question is, ultimately, not what can be made but what produces bodies.

4

Superstars

THE MOVIES ARE GRAVEN IMAGES of mystery and allure. One of the pleasures of moviegoing is watching incandescent people, more intense and riveting, more raffish, witty, and beautiful than the rest of us, defy the special gravity of the screen.

"It's still a matter of excitement, of what people will go to see," says superagent Sue Mengers, whose list of clients includes the *Who's Who* of New Hollywood.

Glamour is neither a misty and endearing past nor a plausible future, but a here-and-now reality. "The star's life *in toto* is a kind of work of art—a sculptured artifice of its own kind," says Peter Bogdanovich, whose cinema is avowedly star-centered. "That's really the iconography of the screen. And that's why I think it's so spurious to discuss whether the star system is or isn't with us anymore."

What moviegoers react to in their special visceral and empathetic way is the appeal of oversized presence. It is the seraphic face of Cathérine Deneuve, the just-rugged-enough handsomeness of Robert Redford, the loose, urban put-on of Dustin Hoffman, the clean-boned, finishing-school unattainability of Ali MacGraw that allow audiences to lose themselves in screen fantasy, to be swept along and get the chills at the final fade-out. Barbra Streisand and Liza Minnelli put the stamp of their personalities on the pictures they make—others don't. George C. Scott *is* Patton. George C. Scott lifted *The Hospital* above television sit-com as Al Pacino lifted *Serpico* above the police "meller" (melodrama) routine. *Easy Rider* lit up the moment Nicholson came on, and *The Godfather* lost voltage the moment Marlon Brando wasn't on the screen. Most of the twenty-seven films of Greta Garbo's extraordinary career are shockingly bad. Don Siegel may be a better director than Ted Post, but *Dirty Harry* and *Magnum Force* are both Clint Eastwood pictures. It has taken Elizabeth Taylor an inordinate number of clunkers to ruin her career. Peter Fonda and Paula Prentiss have never set fire to *any* movie. *M*A*S*H* rescued Donald Sutherland from the ranks of the intriguing-but-anonymous character actors. Dustin Hoffman was ten years too old for the part that made him in *The Graduate*. Carrie Snodgress went from instant stardom in *Diary of a Mad Housewife* to nowhere. John Wayne is a movie star in his seventies, and Lee Marvin suddenly took off in his forty-eighth picture.

Screen presence is mysterious and has been called everything from "it" to chemistry. Since Mutual Film Company began paying Charles Chaplin $10,000 a week in 1916, (when a loaf of bread cost four cents, a luxury apartment rented for $30 a month, and there was no income tax), movie moguls and sociologists have tried to figure out what exactly it is that audiences respond to. No answer is at hand.

It *seems* the basic ingredient in star making is sex appeal, but sex appeal is as difficult to define as stardom itself. What do Twiggy and Maria Schneider, Gene Hackman and Rock Hudson have in common that has to do with sex appeal? Julie Andrews is everybody's tomboy tennis partner, daughter, sister, and mum. Elliott Gould has played louts who are downright offensive to women. After *Blow-Up* and *Camelot* had exposed her sense of presence, mystique and radiance, Vanessa Redgrave was forecast by *Time* to become the Duse of the seventies, but it was Glenda Jackson who became the decade's coping Everywoman, all edge and challenge. Jacqueline Bisset has had a lot of exposure under the guidance of some of the screen's best directors, but has never allowed audiences to discover anything in her performances. Katharine Hepburn seems splendid only when she has an antagonist to play off. Why couldn't Art Garfunkel's pop stardom carry over to the screen? And whatever happened to Peter O'Toole, Genevieve Bujold, and Shirley MacLaine? The gun slingers given equal time in *The Magnificent Seven* were Yul Brynner, Steve McQueen, Horst Bucholz, Charles Bronson, Robert Vaughn, Brad Dexter, and

James Coburn. Ten years later, Brynner was a has-been, McQueen a superstar, Coburn an also-ran, Bucholz and Dexter unknowns, Vaughn a TV commercial actor, and Bronson a *European* star with one obsession: to become an American star.

Actors are the principal victims of the evolution of the movies. Bette Davis may have railed against her gilded bondage at Warner's, and few contemporary stars would submit to the discipline of the contract system, but the system *also* worked in the performers' favor. Actors were valuable properties, and it was to the studios' advantage to further their careers, to develop them and make them last.

"Now a young person makes a hit and with all the instant publicity and everything he or she is declared a star and then goodness knows what that person's next effort will be because new actors don't have the experience to select the right material," says George Cukor. "Also, there is no continuity today; stars have no guarantee that in their next picture they will be well treated and well protected."

Cukor, who directed an extraordinary dozen from Garbo to Garland, including Tallulah Bankhead, Cary Grant, Marilyn Monroe, Norma Shearer, Leslie Howard, Ava Gardner, Audrey Hepburn, Ingrid Bergman, and the Spencer Tracy–Katharine Hepburn classics, feels lasting stardom has to do with talent, looks, intelligence, and character. Self-discipline is necessary both to meet dazzling, overwhelming success and to face bad luck and despair. "You can't have the responsibility of being a star and carrying a great project when you can't control yourself. I've seen very talented people who drink too much or who are careless or plain foolish. Gradually, it affects the circumstances of their career and very often it affects themselves. They're no longer sharp and in command of themselves."

Getting a firm grip on a movie career has always been difficult for an actor, and the very fracturing of filmmaking baffles performers.

"It's amazing what can be done in the cutting room to either hurt or protect an actor," says Dustin Hoffman. "When you do a scene, the director generally takes a master shot, a close-up, and some over-the-shoulder close-ups. If you're an actor who's responsive to the moment, your "takes" will vary, the other actors' takes will vary. When he's finished shooting, the director will whisper to the script girl, 'Print two, four, and six.' You hear this. You feel you did your most interesting work in a take they're not even going to print. Somehow you have to bed the script girl to print it. You feel like a schmuck."

The right to fail has been abbreviated in modern Hollywood. Taking one's temperature every five minutes is not conducive to creativity and compared with triumphant lives of divas of the past—Sarah Bernhardt's career stretched over as many failures as successes—contemporary superstars seem to have narrow, cautious careers.

To George C. Scott, staying power is risking professional failures with offbeat characterizations and cultivating a sense of analysis of himself and his audience. "The audience is a dark thing, a peculiar animal, an enemy that must be assaulted and won. The big competition is there—not between you and the other actors but you and the audience. I think screen acting is also a sense of surprise, knowing how to set up the audience like a great boxer and then give the audience something else. A good actor has a certain consistent style, but his or her individual work can contain enormous variety of color and intelligence."

"Stardom? I can't imagine it," Marisa Berenson said between *Cabaret* and *Barry Lyndon*. "If you want to do this business, you go along."

Young actors are the most pathetic members of the contemporary industry, principally because they lack security, guidance, and initiative. A would-be Fellini making dolly shots in Super 8 on his daughter's tricycle or a writer banging out surreal scripts no one will read are *doing* something. An actor's grip on his own career ends when he has gotten a set of 8-by-10 glossy "composites" of himself and an agent. From there on, meaningful initiative slips out of his hands, and all he can hope for is that the phone rings. When it does and he is called for an audition, it isn't really what he says or does that determines whether he gets the part. All the way up the ladder, casting means fleshing out parts with bodies that conform to production ideas of roles and faces. Only at the top are parts fitted to actors.

Since a young performer must trust someone, he most probably trusts his agent. Yet agents are not his best advisers, insofar as counseling a turndown of a role means money and percentages lost.

A strictly modern pitfall is television. Overexposure on the tube is a kiss of death. "People go to the movies because they can't see Streisand, McQueen, Hackman, Eastwood, and Sidney Poitier on television," says Sue Mengers, whose clients include Streisand, Ryan O'Neal, Cybill Shepherd, Peter Bogdanovich, Dyan Cannon, Gene Hackman, Bob Fosse, Gore Vidal, and Diana Ross. "For the less than top-top names, Movies of the Week pay for the groceries, but doing too much TV ruins big-screen careers. George C. Scott thought he could do it, but had to take a cut in his salary to get back into features. If I handled Burt Reynolds I'd pull him off those talk shows."

In 1974, Redford fought to have himself pulled off the screen. He raised such a stink with Paramount over plans to cash in on his saturation fame with a reissue of *Little Fauss and Big Halsy* that the studio shelved the idea. Before the much-touted premiere of *The Great Gatsby*, Redford was already on the marquees in *The Way We Were*, *The Sting*, and Warner's quickie reissue of *Jeremiah Johnson*.

Underexposure can be just as dangerous. If a star waits too long between assignments, the public may have forgotten. Warren Beatty waited two and a half years after the blockbusting *Bonnie and Clyde*, and both Katharine Ross and Ali MacGraw also failed to capitalize on exciting exposures with follow-up pictures.

Studios are reluctant to gamble superstar salaries on what they consider Movie of the Week material. It *can* be done (Sam Peckinpah's *The Getaway* was given the McQueen-MacGraw treatment), but, goes the reasoning, nobody is going to *pay* to see those familiar faces that flick across the tube every week for free.

Television headliners like to tell themselves that because they are household names they are only one or two juicy roles away from superstardom. Whereas the less-than-first-magnitude actors—Cloris Leachman, Martin Balsam, Cicely Tyson—and identifiable Broadway names like Jason Robards and Julie Harris can float around, television stars *à la* Mary Tyler Moore, Carroll O'Connor, or Bob Newhart would never be considered for "above-title" parts in any feature.

The TV stigma haunts actors from the beginning. Warner Brothers' John Calley gets three hundred telephone calls a day. One hundred of them are from agents. Since he cannot answer all of them, he picks the calls from those he knows. "This is where the 'recognition factor' comes in," says Sue Mengers, who started her own agent's climb in 1967 by throwing elaborate dinner-parties that mixed studio heads with stars, directors, and celebrity authors ("it's a little harder to turn down a call when you had dinner with the caller the night before"). Smaller agents cannot get through to Calley or Gordon Stulberg to recommend "this sensational new actor," and the sensational new actor cannot get on the platinum-covered roster of Sue Mengers, George Chasin, Paul Kohner, or Jack Gilardi because 10 percent of a $5,000 Movie of the Week part cannot command the attention of 10 percent of a $750,000 starring role in a feature. But one of the catch-22 rules for stalking the "impossible dream" is that a new actor's most valuable possession is a strip of film of himself. About the only way to get it is—in television. Astute agents don't try to get auditions for costarring roles with Streisand and McQueen for their promising newcomers but send them to the casting offices of TV series. To know when to stop in television and try for the big-screen "break" is a matter of hunch or non-Euclidean geometry.

"We're basically employment agencies," says Sue Mengers, admitting that *her* 10 percent adds up to nearly half a million dollars a year ("Sue is tops," says client Bogdanovich, "because she has an instinct for judging people who can happen"). Miss Mengers is vice-president of Creative Management Associates (CMA), which, with the William Morris Agency and Marvin Josephson Associates, constitutes the Big Three of talent representatives. William Morris is now almost exclusively in bread-and-butter TV, but Marvin Josephson—better known for its subsidiary, International Famous Agency (IFA)—and CMA also maintain big television departments to help pay for the heavy overhead of superstar representation with its hypersensitive and time-consuming contract negotiations, world-girdling "hand holding" of temperamental actors, and, with deferred payments, long waits for the 10 percent. When Elizabeth Taylor does *Ash Wednesday* for $100,000 in expenses but no "up front" salary, her agent will have to wait something like two years before seeing *his* cut of the actress's percentage of the profit, if any. Film industry bookkeeping is at best Byzantine and at worst downright dishonest.

Superstars *are* overpaid, but inflation is built in. Nobody was paid a million dollars in 1973 (the million dollars-plus paid to McQueen for *Papillon* doesn't really count, since the picture was put together as a French production and non-Hollywood arithmetic applied), but a year later the prices were edging up toward the cool million again. Top stars get between $250,000 and $750,000 per film. Compared with the $100,000 most directors can command—not to talk about the paltry sums most writers get—star salaries *are* crazy, especially when the actors' two months of work is compared to the year the director usually spends on the project.

But holding the line at $750,000—if it can be held—is still fiscal sanity compared to the convulsive million-dollar spins of a few years ago. In 1968, intoxicated by a temporary huge TV market, hypnotized by the vast success of *The Sound of Music, The Graduate, The Odd Couple*, and *Rosemary's Baby*, which together netted $150 million, the studios went off the deep end. Paramount, for example, tied up $50 million in four movies alone. Twentieth Century–Fox offered Taylor and Burton starring roles in *The Only Game in Town* and *Staircase*, respectively. Burton agreed to do his picture and Taylor agreed to do hers provided they could be shot simultaneously in Paris, a city they preferred for a variety of reasons, chiefly tax ones, and provided the studio could afford to pay them $1,250,000 each—a bold increase from their usual million dollars. "The price of food is going up," Miss Taylor said facetiously, "and diamonds, too." She half expected to be turned down and couldn't have cared terribly, but the salaries were met. "Am I surprised producers pay me $1,250,000 a picture?" she told interviewers during shooting. "They must be out of their tiny Chinese minds."

Studio heads now and then attempt to reply. "How we pleaded with those armies of agents and lawyers and tax experts and public relations people, all pushing their prima donnas forward like golden idols while they took their piece off the top," Charles Bluhdorn sighed in a *Look* magazine interview a year later. To which agents answer that nothing forces Paramount or anyone else to pay three-quarters of a million for anyone's eight-week services. Five years later, Columbia agreed to pay James Caan $350,000 to play Fanny Brice's second husband in *Funny Lady*—a lot of money, most agents agreed, considering the continuation of *Funny Girl* is totally a Streisand vehicle.

"Why do we do it?" Columbia's Peter Guber says with a smile. "It's like being at the races. It's human; if you know others are in on it, you want to place a bet, too. Also, when you spend considerable money on the property itself, whether it's a best-selling novel or an original script, you tend to want to go with solid names."

To flesh out their modern stories, directors are obviously looking for people, faces, and attitudes that *look* contemporary. Streisand's specialty has been to destroy the distance between herself and her boisterous persona. By making Jewishness her personal trademark, she seems less typically Jewish—and more modern—than Sylvia Sidney, Judy Holliday, or Fanny Brice, who restrained their mannerisms and intonations and sometimes seemed to carry their Jewishness like a cross. Richard Benjamin, Elliott Gould, and George Segal are the male equivalents, physically well suited to play the urban Jewish heroes who dominated American fiction for over a decade and have now moved onto the screen. Gould always seems to be caught up in social—and sexual—tension and to embody an inner need to be hip at the risk of seeming silly. He couldn't have been a star fifty years ago—just as Valentino would be laughed off the screen today. Whereas urban stars of the 1930s, like John Garfield, were tempered by hard times into resilient, resourceful heroes, the quirky characters Gould, Benjamin, Hoffman, and Segal play frequently seem to need help ordering breakfast.

To star in a Sam Peckinpah movie means playing American Primitives—the colorful saloon hangers-on, subordinate outlaws, and lynch mob trash who in earlier westerns were peripheral characters. Jon Voight, Burt Reynolds, Ned Beatty, and Ronny Cox had to incarnate men with emotional patterns bearing little resemblance to the kind of lives they lead in *Deliverance*. McQueen, Eastwood, and Redford may play winners, but Brando, Hoffman, Nicholson, and others have reached stardom through bravura portrayals of introspective, sympathetic losers.

Male stars have carried the movies during the past few decades, as Pauline Kael says, "not only without much help from women but often without much help from the scripts and the directors." That Streisand is the only actress superstar in the field of McQueen, Redford, Eastwood, Hoffman, Brando, and, in certain things, O'Neal and Newman, is astonishing. Hollywood feminists are quick to accuse the system, chauvinist producers, and/or inept screenwriters. "Right now, there are very few decent roles for women," says Susan Ansprach, who is active in Cine-women, a group putting on workshops for women writers and directors. "Men doing the writing are admitting out loud that they don't know much about women."

"I contend girls' parts are better than boys'," Karen Black told

Newsweek when interviewed for a survey on actresses in contemporary movies. "The 'complexity' of male roles is really made up of simple, basic drives. There are no emotions in conflict—no grief, loss, hysteria, bitterness, or despondency. I think women's roles offer a wider range of emotions. If I were a man I'd always have to be strong and in control." [1]

Most young actresses disagree, saying the women they are asked to flesh out in films are neurotics, sluts, whores, or somebody's daughter. "Love scenes are always done from a man's point of view," says Jacqueline Bisset. "In life when a woman is being sensual it motivates everything she does. In a film she just has to be 'sexy'—it's not attached to anything."

"We're concerned with packaging, not content," says Madeline Kahn. "When they want to focus on my breasts and I say no, they think I have a hangup. But they don't give me any lines to explain my character or show what's in my mind."

Barbra Streisand believes it is all a matter of clout. "There's this prejudice against actresses. They're supposed to look pretty and read their lines, then shut up and go home." Streisand has fought with every director who has directed her but has never gone as far as Steve McQueen, who fired his *Magnificent Seven* director, John Sturges, on *Le Mans* and had him replaced by Lee Katzin.

Superstars can barter their acting services for a chance to direct, and practically all have done it. Paul Newman, for example, did it with *Sometimes a Great Notion, WUSA, Rachel, Rachel,* and *The Effects of Gamma Rays on Man-in-the-Moon Marigolds;* Clint Eastwood directed *Play Misty for Me;* Sidney Poitier directed himself in *Buck and the Preacher, Warm December,* and *Uptown Saturday Night;* Jack Nicholson tried directing with *Drive, He Said.*

After *The Exorcist,* Ellen Burstyn won script approval on *Alice Doesn't Live Here Anymore.* Her first order of business was to change the screenplay, in which she played a single mother earning her living as a singer. "We collaborated between his sense of the dramatic line and my representation of the woman's point of view," she told *Newsweek* about her rewrites with director Martin Scorsese. "We'd write in the margin of the script: 'No, a woman wouldn't do this.' 'Yes, she'd say that.' 'That's not the way.' "

Studio heads have a prosaic explanation for the dearth of women

1. *Newsweek,* Mar. 4, 1974.

superstars: Movies aren't being tailored to women stars because there aren't any. It is not a matter of consciousness raising, they say, pointing to the fact that books and scripts were once snapped up and hand-tooled to accommodate the talents and temperaments of Bette Davis, Joan Crawford, Katharine Hepburn, Merle Oberon, Marlene Dietrich, and Carole Lombard, all formidable ladies who could send ripples of fear through front offices with an arching of an eyebrow.

Indeed, says critic Molly Haskell, women in film have gone from a Golden Age pedestal to utter dehumanization in contemporary porno flicks.

Hollywood writer Linda Gross has a more subtle explanation for the disappearance of the contemporary equivalent of the Bette Davis–Joan Crawford–Katharine Hepburn careers. "Women in America don't identify with superstars but they super-fantasize about them," she says. "Films today reflect a more sophisticated alienation than television, and symbolically Doris Day has gone to TV and become Mary Tyler Moore."

Pauline Kael thinks the fact that male parts outnumber women's roles on the big screen also has to do with modern movies demanding a new, slightly-ahead-of-the-audience kind of acting that only actors with nightclub or cabaret theater training are capable of. Also, since new directors often don't care about performers or don't know how to handle them, acting now means complicity as much as it means learning lines. "Movie acting has been loosening up, and it could be turning into a profession for smarter, more intuitive people," Miss Kael wrote in a 1971 analysis of new actors and acting styles. "Some of the most inventive performances have been in flops—like the performances of Peter Bonerz, the hero of the neglected *Funnyman*, and Berry Primus, the hero of *Been .Down So Long It Looks Like Up to Me*, and William Tepper, the hero of *Drive, He Said*—and so they aren't talked about. But these put-on artists are part of a new and already taken-for-granted style of screen acting, which affects how we look at star-commodity performances. It's now difficult for us to accept the established stars in contemporary settings. We've lived for years with stars who didn't know what to do with a laugh line (has anyone seen Charlton Heston, for example, try to play comedy?)" [2]

2. *New Yorker*, Dec. 4, 1971.

Karen Black is of the opinion that the decline in women's roles reflects the general decline in values. "If you watch old movies on TV," she says, "you see that if the hero lies the girl won't accept him. Now everybody's a thief. Women used to be keepers of the morals. As morals decline, women's roles diminish."

"Nobody's really comfortable right now," says Ellen Burstyn. "It's like musical chairs with everybody asking, 'What chair do I sit in?' "

Clint Eastwood is filmdom's number-one killer and its number-one boxoffice attraction, and he admits he doesn't understand it himself. Redford can play both a woman's man (*The Way We Were, The Great Gatsby*) and a man's man (*Butch Cassidy and the Sundance Kid, The Sting*). Alan Bates says he has always had the urge to play a romantic hero—a Rhett Butler carrying Scarlett O'Hara up the stairway of Tara—but all his career has played witty and mean, yet somehow sympathetic, roles.

If the mechanics of moviemaking no longer favor performers and the industry is only indirectly star-oriented, social trends nevertheless allow today's actors a freer, more honest, and more amplified self-projection than was possible for Golden Era stars. Over the last decade, the movies have bounced from the barricades to the bedroom, and in order to "reach the tribes," they have become seductive, full of light reflected in shiny surfaces, full of foul-mouthed close-ups, Dionysian anarchism, and spunky displays of youth's strength, appeal, and power. For actors it has meant a new sense of complicity in the creative process. Also—and this may have helped the men especially—new life-styles have allowed more striking, flamboyant, and assertive fashions in dress, style, and behavior that have also helped create romantic heroes.

Most contemporary stars are ambivalent about their work and image. "Who *is* Barbra Streisand anyway?" she asks in interviews. She was genuinely baffled by the failure of *Up the Sandbox*—produced by the First Artists company she, McQueen, Hoffman, Newman, and Poitier formed to keep their careers going. *Sandbox*, directed by Irvin Kershner, was the first film over which she exercised any measure of control. "I enjoy seeing some of my ideas come to life, but now I'm interested in my career only to a degree. I'm still me, but I may change."

In their more introspective moments, stars suffer the familiar agony of those who have risen high but can't understand the forces that lifted them. They see psychoanalysts to find answers and comprehend "the real me."

Redford says few roles fit him. "I'm constantly wrestling with issues as a person, my feelings about America, about the environment, the system. And I believe in working out that struggle in film." Eastwood is for gun control even if he snuffs out lives in a dispassionate, remorseless fashion on the screen. He thinks luck has been the major factor in his career. Benjamin says he has never wanted to be the person he usually plays. "You take what you can get, and hopefully you get smarter," he said with a grin during the filming of *Westworld*. "I'd like to be the strong hero type. You know, the guy who saves all the orphans."

5

Hot Scripts

"THE CINEMA," Graham Greene observed at the time of *The Third Man*, "has always developed by means of a certain low cunning." Today Hollywood has lost many of its terrors and kept a fair amount of its charm, and Dorothy Parker's claim that it was necessary to sell soul, integrity, and genius to the Philistines of old Hot Siberia is somehow a little passé. Hollywood is a place where a writer can be what he is and what he wants, where he can make a respectable six figures in one year and work the next for $480 a month as a university assistant teacher.

A number of expensive flops have brought a switch in emphasis, and the raw material that counts in the executive offices is *also* original scripts written by hip young unknowns. Hollywood cynics don't totally agree. "Whatever sells will go," says *Daily Variety* editor A. D. Murphy. "When *Doctors' Wives* and the latest Jacqueline Susann adaptation bomb but *Shaft* makes millions, everybody is in favor of originals. When *Day of the Jackal* makes it big, studios are looking at 'presold' properties again."

Broadway successes and best-selling novels were considered to be "presold" screen material, even if the prices were often inflationary. *Rosemary's Baby* is the classic example. When the witchcraft thriller was still in manuscript, William Castle bought the rights for $100,000—with an additional $50,000 to Ira Levin if his book reached best sellerdom. The *Rosemary's Baby* Roman Polanski filmed for $2.3 million earned $30 million worldwide. Powerful Broadway musicals are traditionally more expensive than novels, but the yields can be commensurate. Warner Brothers paid a whopping $5.5 million for the rights to *My Fair Lady* (after the Alan Jay Lerner–Frederick Loewe musicalization of Bernard Shaw's *Pygmalion* had run for more than a thousand Broadway performances) and shelled out another $12 million filming it, but saw the domestic gross reach $34 million.

What soured corporate Hollywood on "hot properties" are such financial flops as *Topaz*, *The Salzburg Connection*, *Portnoy's Complaint*, and *The Other*—all at one time at the top of the best-seller charts—and such Broadway adaptations as *Hello, Dolly!*, *Mame*, *Last of the Red Hot Lovers*, *Child's Play*, and *40 Carats*. The time-lag between literary best sellerdom and release of a movie version is a continuous peril—and entirely production companies' own fault. The reasons for the failure of screen versions are not always imputable to their literary and/or theatrical origins. Gene Kelly's version of *Hello, Dolly!* was simply too expensive to recoup its cost. The *Mame* Gene Saks directed for Warner's opened to little better than 50 percent of the first week of WB's 1972 comedy hit, *What's Up, Doc?* directed by Peter Bogdanovich. The *Portnoy's Complaint* Ernest Lehman directed had too little of the Philip Roth original to satisfy any public. *Topaz* was simply not vintage Hitchcock, and the *Salzburg Connection* Lee Katzin made of Helen MacInnes' suspense novel turned out to be a routine Nazi melodrama. A generational chasm separates the audience enjoying Neil Simon comedies and people grooving on movies.

Even if pulp masters like Arthur Hailey and Harold Robbins don't always find takers—Hailey's *Wheels* didn't become a movie and Robbins' *The Betsy* only made it to TV pilotdom—studios still buy expensive novels. From the stage, they have bought such West End–Broadway hits as *Hadrian VII*, *After the Fall*, *Armageddon*, *Coco*, and *Rosencrantz and Guildenstern Are Dead*, all expensive and promising plays that somehow turned out to be unwieldy and were shelved.

"Another reason we're shying away from hot properties today is that there's a long way from novel or play to script," says Columbia's Peter Guber. "All things being equal, I'd rather go with a screenplay than a novel because once a project is in script form, whether it's an original or an adaptation, you're already over so many hurdles."

The cliffhanger of literary classics never licked and abandoned on the eve of one scheduled production is *Man's Fate*. Sergei Eisenstein was the first would-be director of an adaptation of André Malraux's 1933 novel about revolution in China, and Fred Zinnemann was the last. Work was halted on the Carlo Ponti–Fred Zinnemann *Man's Fate* in November 1969, three days before principal photography was to start in London and Singapore. An estimated $4 million had already been spent on the $8-to-$10 million MGM production, a budget James Aubrey simply vetoed as too expensive when he took over. He maintained that the liability belonged to the Ponti-Zinnemann company formed for the film, and a welter of suits followed. Two screenwriters, a complete cast (including David Niven, Peter Finch, Liv Ullmann, Max von Sydow, and Eiji Okada), sets, and costumes all contributed to the huge preproduction costs.

Aubrey did try to save the production, but Ponti and Zinnemann claimed his options were impossible to meet. One, aimed at tightening Metro's direct control over the expensive production, would have made Zinnemann responsible to MGM. The other option was for Ponti to guarantee any budget overrun and the completion of the film. This led to a lengthy meeting in New York between Ponti's American lawyer, Lee Steiner, Zinnemann, MGM distribution vice-president Douglas Netter, and a representative of the William Morris Agency. The meeting broke up—and *Man's Fate* was shelved—when Steiner (for Ponti) and Zinnemann declined to go along. Three days later, Zinnemann blasted MGM's cancelation as "a wanton disregard of obligations entered into freely and eagerly by the company," and Von Sydow and Miss Ullmann filed breach-of-contract suits, claiming MGM had entered into oral agreement with them to costar, at $150,000 for Von Sydow and $200,000 for Miss Ullmann, plus transportation and expenses. In 1972, former UMC Pictures production chief Sidney Glazier expressed interest in *Man's Fate*, still owned by MGM, partially because his mother-in-law was authoress Han Suyin, one of the scripters of the Ponti-Zinnemann screen version. Six months later, Ponti thought he had a deal which would make *Man's Fate* the first Italian-Chinese coproduction, with all locations in China. In 1974, when MGM settled the breach-of-contract suits with Zinnemann, Von Sydow, and Miss Ullmann, former Paramount executive Peter Bart and British director Karel Reisz announced plans to reactivate the project.

Other famous novels and plays that were bought but never reached the screen include Franz Werfel's *Forty Days of Musa Dagh*, John Steinbeck's *The Winter of Our Discontent*, (both MGM properties), John Updike's *Couples* (UA), Arthur C. Clarke's science fiction classic *Childhood's End* (Universal), Arthur Miller's *After The Fall* (Paramount), and Bruce Jay Friedman's *Scuba Duba*. William Styron's 1967 best seller, *The Confessions of Nat Turner*, is possibly the best example of precipitate snapping up of literary properties. Bought for an inflated $600,000—a record base price for film rights in 1967—the book ran into immediate opposition from black leaders who claimed the novel "murdered the spirit of one of the great ethnic heroes of black Americans." Norman Jewison withdrew from the project. Sidney Lumet was on *Nat Turner* for a while until producer David Wolper and Fox quietly dropped the whole thing.

Smooth-talking literary agents can still flimflam studios out of six-figure sums, collect their 10 percent, and run before touted best sellerdom fizzles. In 1974 Universal cast wary glances at the poor business Paramount's *The Friends of Eddie Coyle* did at the boxoffice, since it had just handed *Coyle* novelist George V. Higgins $175,000 for the rights to his follow-up tome, *The Digger's Game*. Also, Dorothy Uhnak's *Law and Order*, sold to Paramount for $350,000 when the police yarn was still in galleys, failed to live up to its advance billing in bookstores.

That sanity *can* prevail is seen in the decision by Fox and Warner's to be partners rather than rivals when they found themselves owners of virtually similar properties about fire in a high-rise office building. In 1973 Fox paid $400,000 for the screen rights to *The Glass Inferno*, by Thomas N. Scortia and Frank Robinson, while WB paid $300,000 for Richard Martin Stern's *The Tower*, another novel about disaster in an office building. Stirling Silliphant was signed to write a screenplay from material in both books, which at the combined cost of $700,000 rank second only to the $1.5 million Columbia paid for Jacqueline Susann's *The Love Machine*.

Fox, who had made a fortune on Miss Susann's first novel, *Valley of the Dolls*, bid $1 million for *The Love Machine* but was turned down, as was a mutual fund offering $4.7 million for film, TV, sound-track recording, second-serial, and a portion of the paperback rights. Such multimedia deals tend to feed on each other: Paperback sales influence the movie sale, which, in turn, influences

"The newest trend is that both ends of 'talent' —directors and stars—come together before the project gets to the studio." Above: Jack Nicholson in the "together" *The Fortune*.

The works of some of America's most talented filmmakers never see the inside of *any* studio. Left: Robert Altman with Warren Beatty during the filming of *McCabe and Mrs Miller*.

Most powerful man in the business: Lew Wasserman.

Exploitation cum profits: AIP's Samuel Z. Arkoff.

Above: Passionate attempts at New Things: Stan Van Der Beek in the "magic/movie/space/theater" called *Movie-Drome*.

Below: A scene from the never-heard-from-again filmmaker Charles Eastman's never-released *The All-American Boy*, starring Jon Voight.

Lifting the material above the routine: Al Pacino as *Serpico*, with Tony Roberts.

Risking professional failure with offbeat characterizations: George C. Scott as a Nazi in *Hindenburg*.

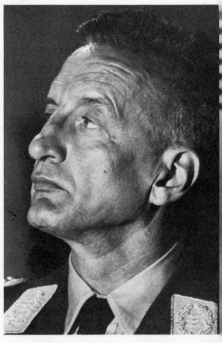

"People go to the movies because they can't see Streisand, McQueen, Hackman, Eastwood, and Sidney Poitier on television."

Steve McQueen in *The Towering Inferno*.

Above: Gene Hackman in Marseilles in *The French Connection II*.

Below: Barbra Streisand with director Herbert Ross on *Funny Lady*.

Sidney Poitier in *Uptown Saturday Night*.

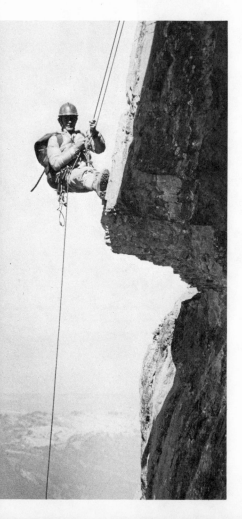

Clint Eastwood in *The Eiger Sanction*.

Robert Redford in *The Great Waldo Pepper*.

foreign rights sales. "You can't manufacture a best seller," New York agent Scott Meredith (Norman Mailer, Spiro Agnew) says, "but you can sure start the ball rolling."

The emphasis, however, is shifting away from costly best sellers and stage hits to original screenplays, written by people who have a sense of what "under thirty" audiences want—often recent graduates of cinema departments of big-city universities, who are increasingly turning to writing because words on paper are a commodity understood well by commodity-conscious studios.

John Milius is one.

At twenty-eight, Milius is a burly gun expert, champion surfer, health freak, and gourmet who sold *The Life and Times of Judge Roy Bean* to Paul Newman for $300,000 (domestic gross, $7 million) and then elbowed himself into directing another of his scripts, *Dillinger*.

"They're outbidding each other," says the stocky writer-director who calls himself Hollywood's resident expert in legendary Americans. A graduate of the University of Southern California (USC) film school, Milius got himself a job at American International Pictures and wrote the motorcycle picture *The Devil's 8*. It was followed by four other original scripts—*Jeremiah Johnson*, *Evil Knieval*, *The Life and Times of Judge Roy Bean*, and *Magnum Force*—before he got to direct the violent *Dillinger*.

"The last thing they want is television hacks," he says, adding that the silliest thing a new screenwriter can do is ape others. "My pictures are sentimental, idealistic. Nobody writes movies in the style I do. I deal with friendships, chivalry, honor, and courage—not just 'guts.' "

Younger than Milius are Paul Schrader and David S. Ward. Warner's bought Schrader's *Yakuza*, a satire on an older American hood in the Tokyo underworld, which Robert Aldrich was to direct with Lee Marvin but dropped when Robert Mitchum became Warner's leading man (and Sidney Pollack took over as director). Price: $300,000 and a percentage of the profits. AIP, hardly noted for lavish up-front money, set an in-house record by paying Schrader $50,000 plus percentages for his rape-themed *Rolling Thunder*, and Columbia bought his science fiction script, *Close Encounter of the Third Kind*, for *Jaws* director Steve Spielberg and spent more than $200,000 on *Taxi Driver* for Martin Scorsese, while independent producer George Litto bought *Déjà Vu* to star Genevieve

Bujold for director Brian De Palma. Ward was two years out of UCLA when he sold *The Sting* to producers Tony Bill and Michael and Julia Phillips.

"*The Sting* was shot very much as I wrote it," he said when he picked up the 1973 screenwriting Oscar for his effort. "The action and dialogue are much the same, only the tone is a bit different. It's more lighthearted, because of George Roy Hill's style of directing. I'm a big fan of the film."

Ward spent five months researching *The Sting*, working at the downtown L.A. public library, tracking down retired con men, and talking with bunko squad policemen. It took him nearly as long to write the script. "No one would let me direct it because it was a period film and therefore more expensive." No one would trust Ward with the direction of his first script, *Steelyard Blues*, a zany comedy edged in black. It was directed by Alan Myerson, the founding father of San Francisco's The Committee (whose members filled most of the subsidiary roles behind Jane Fonda, Donald Sutherland, and Peter Boyle). "*Steelyard* suffered from too many separate visions and a large amount of inexperience on our parts, but we all learned from it and that is important."

Ward told a USC film conference symposium in 1974 that his two screenplays were more socially conscious than the two films made from them, and that if he had directed *The Sting*, the movie would have been totally different, although perhaps not as commercially successful. "But there's a point when it's counterproductive to force your concepts on the director."

After *The Sting*'s runaway success, Ward was at work on two originals, one on the brutal life of hard-rock miners in the 1870s and a contemporary project which he would direct about a professional lady gambler. "I can direct the gambler picture because it can be done on a small budget."

"I'm kind of proletarian," says Ward, who got a commitment from his producers (Tony Bill and the Phillipses also produced *Steelyard Blues*) on the basis of his briefly telling the story of *The Sting*. "I'm interested in working people, people with limited choices and not much leisure, how people for whom freedom will never be a reality retain their dignity."

Another "under thirty" success is Tom Rickman, who in 1973 alone sold three originals, including *W. W. and the Dixie Danceking*, filmed a year later with John Avildsen directing and Burt Reynolds starring. Other hefty sales are a reputed $300,000 going to Carol Eastman (*Five Easy Pieces*) for her *The Fortune*, bought jointly by Mike Nichols, Warren Beatty, and Jack Nicholson, and the $300,000 plus juicy percentages paid Robert Towne for his *Chinatown* original (and $150,000 for his adaptation of Darryl Ponicsan's novel *The Last Detail*).

"People want to escape into stories with strong narrative lines," Towne said after writing *Shampoo* for Beatty. "A well-made screenplay has to go somewhere, not just ramble around. A good script should have air in it, to allow everybody latitude. If you don't want to totally alienate directors and actors and drive them crazy, don't tell them what they're feeling."

Young couples moving in are Gail Parent (*Sheila Levine Is Dead and Living in New York*) and Kenny Solms, who wrote for the Carol Burnett show for four years, and Gloria Katz and Willard Huyck (*American Graffiti*).

The Katz-Huyck wife-husband team were contracted a year in advance after *American Graffiti* for their original, *Lucky Lady*, which may eventually yield them more money than William Goldman's *Butch Cassidy and the Sundance Kid* (at $400,000 the previous all-time high for an original). The terms for *Lucky Lady*, directed by Stanley Donen for Fox and starring Liza Minnelli, call for them to receive between $300,000 and $450,000 plus participation points.

They are eager to get all of the writing done because the last of the string of projects—one they have signed with Columbia's "new math" executive producer Lawrence Gordon (late of AIP, as are the Huycks)—is their ultimate goal because Willard will direct and Gloria produce it.

"I think we all love movies, learned to love them as kids and continued all the way through school," says Huyck. "We want to make good films, to entertain people. Most of the people we've met have really been decent. Many of us are friends. It's so hard to make a film it's foolish to make it with people you don't like."

Ward, the Huycks, Milius, and most of the other under-thirty newcomers aren't angry rebels. "The previous generation, like Hopper and Fonda, wanted to destroy the American movie," Ward told the USC writers' symposium, also attended by the Huycks and Milius. "There is a social responsibility in filmmaking, but we avoid it," Milius told the five hundred students attending. "It's sad that our movies aren't really about anything. I hope we develop

into the kind of directors who make movies about something."
Gloria Katz said the studios desperately want blockbusters, which
makes it even more difficult for the smaller, riskier film. They all
agreed that for any film with a budget over $2 million the use of
stars becomes a necessity, although all big stars have made flops.

Being man and wife, Gloria and Willard gleefully agree, allows
them to fight well beyond the normal writing partners' arguments,
and to fight dirtier. They live in an art deco home in the Hollywood hills, but do their writing in a book-lined office beneath their
hillside home—Willard sitting at a traditional desk while she faces
him from a sort of sit-down pulpit. Their speciality is comedy,
they told Wayne Warga of the Los Angeles Times in 1974, "because
comedy is instant gratification and film is best when it enter-
tains." [1]

"We want to be successful," says Huyck. "There is competition
among all of us who are from the film schools and in the business
now. We all suggest one another for jobs. Francis Ford Coppola has
helped many of us, as have others."

They all wrote socially conscious screenplays—all unsold, before
their more lighthearted, escapist scripts brought them success.
American Graffiti was a two-year odyssey, which only got made
because Coppola agreed to become executive producer. "Faith has a
lot to do with making movies," Gloria says. "American Graffiti was
developed at United Artists but finally turned down. We took it
every place and got turned down. AIP got interested, but wouldn't
commit. Universal's vice-president Ned Tanen liked the script, but
said we had to get Francis involved." When Coppola lent his name
and Tanen became the driving force behind the project, the
Huycks, who wrote the original treatment with George Lucas,
completely rewrote the screenplay.

The love of movies isn't as pronounced among successful, older
Hollywood scribes. More abused and cynical than the junior
screenwriters, they seem not to be able to make up their minds
whether to use the clout that comes with success to get more
money or, like their younger confreres, to use their bargaining
power to get a chance to direct.

Screenwriters *are* underrated, and their jealousy of directors and
intense desire to establish creative identity are understandable if not

1. *Los Angeles Times*, Feb. 9, 1974.

legitimate. Few of them, however, will work "on spec," i.e., write on speculation as the novelists they want to emulate normally do and *then* sell their creation. A writer with a few hits to his credit is more likely to ask his agent to find him a studio with a best seller it wants to have adapted then to retire to his typewriter for six months and, once the dream project is finished, negotiate a deal from a position that allows him to ask for more than money.

All screenwriters sooner or later get involved in abortive projects and in rewriting each other's scripts. For every screenplay actually filmed, each writer has at least ten stillborn efforts, and each script reaching the screen has gone through several revisions. A project *everybody* seems to have worked on is *Choice Cuts* by Pierre Boileau and Thomas Narcejac, a pair of Frenchmen who wrote the novel that *Vertigo* was based on. *Choice Cuts* is about transplants, and no scripter has licked it. Most writers, it seems, feel the subject is funny, while Warner's insists the end-result should be scary and horrifying.

Control over the material is the prime concern of screenwriters, and most agree that slow headway is being made, if not in legal terms at least in respect for the writer's work. Still, scripts are treated appallingly. They are the property of whoever forms the producing company and can be torn up and rewritten *ad infinitum*. Typically, when Paul Newman joined the cast of *The Towering Inferno*, Stirling Silliphant was called back to rework the script so as to make Newman's role no less than Steve McQueen's.

The hallmark of screenwriting, as *Film Comment* editor Richard Corliss has remarked, is versatility, not consistency, because subject matter dictates style. The writers who adapted their talents to the Byzantine demands of the trade have always been rewarded in princely fashion. Golden Era moguls like Samuel Goldwyn and David Selznick openly courted writers, and such thirties and forties Hollywood writers as Ben Hecht, Sidney Buchman, Frances Marion, Howard Koch, Jo Swerling, Frank S. Nugent, and Anita Loos pulled down $2,000-a-week assignments fifty weeks a year. Selznick paid Hecht $15,000 for one week's frantic rewriting of Sidney Howard's *Gone with the Wind* script. Miss Loos was in the highest bracket of writer salaries from 1922 to 1942.

The emergence of the director as the creative focal point has left older writers bitter and young scripters itching to become directors. "The screenwriter knows that there is nothing more ludicrous than a director without a screenplay he can *auteur*, like a Don Juan without a penis," oldtimer Carl Foreman could write in 1970.[2] Others can quote chapter and verse on directors who not only fail to add anything, but often diminish or cheapen what is on paper. Younger writers take screenwriting as a way-station to other and better things. Successful scripters gain increasing control over their material by becoming "hyphenates"—writer-producers, writer-directors, or writer-director-producers—or, in the opposite direction, they retire to the solitary profession of the novelist.

"The directing of a film, to me, is simply an extension of the process of writing," says John Huston, who successfully made the transition from writing to directing nearly forty years ago. "It's the process of rendering the thing you have written. You're still writing when you're directing. Of course you're not composing words, but a gesture, the way you make somebody raise his eyes or shake his head is also writing for films."

Today's young screenwriters are riding in on the most powerful of crests—the youth wave—although veteran scripters such as Waldo Salt (*Midnight Cowboy, The Day of the Locust*) and Ring Lardner, Jr. (*M*A*S*H*) have learned to meet the demands of the youth market.

Increasingly, it has occurred to the Wassermans, the Stulbergs, and the Dillers that the people who see Broadway dramas and read best sellers are not necessarily the people who go to the movies. The annual Opinion Research Corporation survey for the Motion Picture Producers' Association (MPPA) varies slightly in percentage figures, but the message reads loud and clear: Three-quarters of all moviegoers in America are between twelve and twenty-nine years of age. Two-thirds of those with some college education go often, and frequent moviegoers provide almost nine-tenths of all admissions. Given the original populist base of the movies as *the* mass medium, the profile of today's moviegoer as young and well-educated shows not so much a gentle shift as a revolutionary change.

2. *Film Comment*, winter 1970–71.

6

"Winner Take All"

As THEY SAY on credit crawls, all characters and situations in this chapter are fictitious even if they bear an astonishing resemblance to very real characters and situations. The reason is not fear of treble-damage suits, but to dramatize the fine art of package making. Packaging is the most important activity in contemporary moviemaking and tends to absorb so much ingenuity, energy, and plain man-hours that the actual making of the resulting film is almost anticlimactic. Severe critics of filmmaking American-style rightfully point out that all the sweat shifts the emphasis from end-result to deal making.

At Perfect Packagers one bright morning, the head of the literary department phones PP himself to tell him he has just read a terrific script, *Winner Take All*, which one of their writer-clients has just turned in. The "property," says the agent, is just right for Steve McQueen and Karen Black, both of whom are Perfect Packagers clients and not adverse to getting work.

"What's it about?"

"*Bonnie and Clyde* with a kind of nice twist."

In the eternity of the next five seconds, fate hangs in the balance for the first time but certainly not the last. "*Bonnie and Clyde* with a kind of nice twist" is an insult to the writer's integrity and angst, but a cat is a cat is a cat. The need for pigeonholing and labeling is no more demeaning in filmdom than in any other collective enterprise. What the boss is weighing during his five seconds' silence is whether anybody will be interested in a *"Bonnie and Clyde* with a nice twist," whether the project has the chance of getting *any* attention.

If after reading it PP agrees that *Winner Take All* is indeed viable—meaning that he thinks it's the kind of project currently in demand—the packaging begins. So far no money has changed hands, and none will for quite a while. If *Winner Take All* is an original, the writer has written it "on spec." If it's an adaptation of a novel—a novel, that is, which isn't the hottest number on the best-seller charts—a few thousand dollars will have been spent by someone, not necessarily the screenwriter, on an option on the literary source material.

There are two ways of bankrolling *Winner Take All:* 1) by raising outside money; or 2) through a deal with a major such as Warner's, Paramount, or Columbia. Few promoters have been successful in raising money independently. Nonindustry money accounts for only 5 percent of all movie financing, and more often than not it is raised under false pretexts—alleged tax shelters or write-offs—and is notoriously skittish and unreliable. Making a distribution deal with a major means the film will be made with the distributor's money (see Chapter 9).

Before knocking on any Paramount, Columbia, or United Artists executive door, Perfect Packagers must have a "package," a royal flush of property, director, star, and schedule that is irresistible. Many hardened packagers are convinced that the majors must be given no excuse to say no, that the whole art lies in forcing their hand, for example by making them spend so much "development money" that they will have to wade in.

"Bonnie and Clyde with a nice twist" obviously brings to mind Arthur Penn, but he is not necessarily interested in repeating himself by making another "gangster classic." And anyway, McQueen and Penn have never worked together. Nothing says it has to be Perfect Packagers client McQueen, of course, or Karen Black. It would just be nice for PP, since the agency could then collect 10 percent many times around.

Names get kicked around. The package can change indefinitely, and probably will. Michael Ritchie is a good young director who has worked with Robert Redford twice, with Gene Hackman and

Lee Marvin, although his track record is somewhat limited in what he has done. *Winner Take All*—by now abbreviated to *Winner* or *WTA* in agency shop talk—may interest Ritchie, who in turn may attract his own talent.

Perfect Packagers feels its way around. Television directors who have never worked with really big names are difficult to package, and the hottest directors—the Bogdanoviches, the Coppolas—develop their own properties and are usually not for hire.

All options are open. In a rewrite, the emphasis can be shifted from *Winner Take All*'s Clyde to its Bonnie, or adjustments can be made to accommodate Dick Benjamin's persona or Richard Harris' speech patterns. If Raquel Welch has seen the critically acclaimed work of a director who perhaps hasn't done much, if she has been impressed with what he has done in a certain picture—this is the newcomer's biggest chance—the package may turn that way. This director may not be a big name, but if Perfect Packagers can go to Paramount and say, "With him we've got *her*," a deal may fall into place very quickly. Despite all the sound and fury, directors—with the exception of Alfred Hitchcock—don't really sell tickets.

No matter how great *Winner Take All* is, no matter how much perfection the writer has brought to it, rewrites are inevitable. The first time PP brings its package to Warner's, the best possible answer it can get is, 'Fine, we like the idea. Let's develop it a little.' This decision opens the purse strings for the first time. "Seed money," usually between $15,000 and $20,000, becomes available. This kind of one-step-at-a-time involvement by the studio is a sensible way for developing a project. Paramount, Warner's, UA, *et al.* have been burned once too often to go for "open-ended" deals.

The contract to develop the first draft is between the major and PP, and the revision may not go to the original *Winner* writer. Rewrites, however, keep Writers' Guild of America members alive collectively. Everybody, it seems, is always rewriting somebody else's script.

Since PP cannot afford to sit idle for four or five weeks while *WTA* is given a polishing job, it has other projects going. PP needs five or six projects that it feels it has faith in, because *Winner* may be the project nobody wants now.

To strengthen its hand and to skip the expense of one rewrite, PP may postpone the script revisions until the director is brought in. If *Winner* is in its fourteenth draft when the director comes aboard, there will be a fifteenth. His ego and artistic machismo demand that.

So far we have assumed that everybody is equally available. The next storey in the house of cards is scheduling. Ritchie may be the director, and Lee Marvin the star who will want to make *Winner* with Ritchie, and Warner's John Calley may like the combination, but suppose that Marvin is not free when Ritchie is and that when Ritchie becomes available the actor is tied up. Here comes another crucial decision: "Go further down the line" or mothball the package? Not only greed favors the first solution, since packages wither easily. If any amount of time goes by, the deal with Warner's may collapse, and even if everything could be mothballed for twelve months there is no guarantee that the ingredients will stay together in a year's time. Nobody is in business until *all* direct commitments are signed.

The second, third, and fourth choices are never called that. If there is one law of the Golden Era that is still being observed, it is the practice of never announcing anything until after the scrawl on the dotted line. Before announcing that Goldie Hawn will costar with Lee Marvin in Warner Brothers' *Winner Take All*, Ritchie, PP, and WB may go through a descending order of Dyan Cannon, Marisa Berenson, Sarah Miles, Candice Bergen, Genevieve Bujold, Lindsay Wagner, and Diane Keaton, but the industry and the public at large will never know. Who would have enjoyed the movies if they had known that Natalie Wood was the first singing-novice choice for *The Sound of Music*, that Sir Laurence Olivier at one point was considered for the title role in *The Godfather*, that Robert Redford was not the original choice for the Sundance Kid? Despite the foibles and eccentricities actors have always been accused of, they all have enough sense of self-preservation to observe the rule and just smile to talk-show hosts asking *what* picture they are up for, or brush off fans' queries with, "I'm much too superstitious to tell you." The practice is by and large observed among directors also. Nobody is supposed to know that Roman Polanski was an early choice to direct *The Day of the Dolphin* or that *Serpico* was a John Avildsen picture before it became a Sidney Lumet film.

From scheduling we go on to the minefield of total ego. The choice of Goldie Hawn over Dyan or Marisa is not only a matter of availability. It is also a question of the highly emotional mathemat-

ics of price as measured against the constantly shifting scale of popularity. This seesaw of financial considerations and drawing power
is not for the faint-hearted. Cynics have blushed at hearing how
little "names" will sometimes work for. This is the world of "When
you're hot, you're hot," of artful knifings in the back, of ampheta-
mine comebacks, cheerful sellouts and "Nobody's better than his
last flop, kid." This is the raw-nerved fantasy-brothel that is being
mined by pulp fiction.

In reality, it's just PP, Ritchie, and Warner's packaging, measur-
ing "above-the-line" costs against the overall *Winner* budget. It's
asking, What kind of talent can we get for how much? Why pay
Dyan $250,000 when we can get Sarah for a hundred grand and
Genevieve for $25,000? What will happen if we go with Candy?
How's the chemistry if we go with Karen Black, after all? And any-
way, what's Lee's last figure? Suppose we went with Karen and
Jack Nicholson? What about casting deliberately against type—
Karen as a ballsy Bonnie and Peter Finch as a classy Clyde? Far
out!

Successful movies are much more "chemistry"—incandescent
and sometimes unsuspected combinations—than raw money, and
all possibilities are advanced and explored. Lee Marvin can be out
and James Coburn in—and out—of contention in one afternoon of
high-adrenalin telephone calls to their agents. Elliott Gould would
give the hero a forlorn, slogging-along kind of character, Burt Reynolds would give everything a romantic charge, Nicholson would
give it bluster and self-kidding machismo.

Tailing each other in and out of the production office are the talent agents, each cajoling and bargaining. The con is as thick as at
an Armenian thieves' market, and more than one star has accused
his agent of being his worst enemy. Some ten percenters have
jacked a client's price up so high when the actor was hot that he
never got a second chance; others have wasted promising stars by
talking them into accepting a series of clunkers. After *A Man and a
Woman*, Jean-Louis Trintignant and Anouk Aimée were both
swamped. He took anything and everything. Her agent suggested
selectivity: big American prestige vehicles. Ten years later, he was
a recognizable international name despite the string of Italian Z
movies and despite turning down *Last Tango in Paris*. After such
million-dollar efforts as George Cukor's lame *Justine*, she was a has-
been.

The heady highwire act of considering the possibilities cannot go on forever. The scrabble must spell out something or there is no deal. All other things being equal, what clinches Gould over Marvin and brings the part back to Karen may actually be a matter of mutually agreeable figures. Stars can no longer submit conditions on how many hours they will work, or how close their dressing-room trailer must be to the actual shooting, but an actor or actress in demand carries a lot of clout and a sharp agent can still drive insane deals. Nevertheless, as Charles Bluhdorn has said, "A great script and a devoted director, that's what makes things happen."

Beyond percentages of eventual profits, inducements to Gould and Karen Black may include another rewrite and a change of title. Once into production, distributors hate to change titles, since whatever publicity is garnered for *Winner Take All* during filming is lost if it comes out as *Loser Drop All*.[1]

The final price tag can still change everything. What interests Warner's at $2.3 million may not interest the company at $3.2 million. The traditional break-even point for a movie is 2.7 times its cost, meaning that at $2.3 million *Winner Take All* will have to gross $6.2 million before Warner's, PP, or anyone else "participating" see their first dollar. At $3.2 million, it will have to pull in $8.6 million. At an average ticket price of $2.50 (between first run and drive-in grind), that means two and a half million more people will have to see it to reach the magic break-even point. That's more customers than a Broadway smash hit sees in a year.

Unlike French wines, however, packages travel well. What doesn't interest Warner's may interest Columbia in relation to *its* line-up of films in release, before the cameras, and in development. Retitled *Straight Aces*, the project may still end up behind the Columbia lady with her flaming torch.

Before Columbia signs the commitment, the package is reevaluated on its own merit. The ingredients, the budget, the professional approach of PP, the safeguards to make sure the production does come in, the kind of people the director has in mind for *behind* the camera, the schedule, and the locations are all analyzed. If Lloyd's of London has lost a bundle insuring a Ritchie picture that went ten weeks over, or a Gould-starrer scratched midway through

---

1. Such 180-degree title switches are not uncommon. Nervousness over drug-themed films in 1971 had UA change the title of Ivan Passer's first American film from *Scraping Bottom* to *Born to Win*, and MGM changed Stuart Hagman's *Speed Is of the Essence* to *Believe in Me*.

filming because of his illness, little red flags go up and the package is dead.

In this simplified example, the whole thing started with a script at the Perfect Packagers agency, but the "first initiative" can start anywhere. A director can read a book and get excited enough to start his own packaging. A star who feels her career plateau now demands a dark romantic vehicle or a zany comedy can find the ideal property; a studio executive can react to a trend; and a lawyer, representing a number of these people, can unscramble messages crossing his desk. The possibilities are limitless, although the *kind* of property that commands attention is limited. Nobody will waste time and efforts on a property lacking popular potential. To get to first base, a property must look financially viable up front.

What about the producer?

The packager *is* the producer.

7

Directors' Lib

THE HOLLYWOOD DIRECTOR may no longer dress up for the part, sport puttees and wield riding crops, but once the cameras are rolling he is the person in charge. The image of the cigar-chomping producer hiring and firing directors and putting nubile nymphettes into *his* picture belongs, again, to overheated fiction.

As with civil rights, the director's liberation has been less a matter of emotions than of law and public awareness, and his triumph is now duly codified in collective agreements. "Between the time the director is employed and until the time he delivers the 'director's cut' and provided the director is reasonably available, he shall participate in all decisions with respect to all creative elements in the production of the film, including but not restricted to the script and any revision thereof, casting, employment of the artistic or creative personnel, rights of approval granted to third parties; location selection, set design, construction, preproduction, shooting, etc.," reads a section of the current contract between the Association of Motion Picture and Television Producers and the Directors' Guild of America.

The director has not yet achieved the millennium—the final cut—but he is almost there, and has come full circle to reemerge with the romance and glamour of his pioneering forefathers.

"They were marvelous men, these silent-picture makers," said David O. Selznick in the 1950s. "They had no affectations, they were full of adventure and the desire to do things. They were impatient and made their pictures very quickly. They were extremely imaginative and knowledgeable. They were a wonderful breed."

The director was always there, the original jack-of-all-trades and, with the cameraman, the original technician. The cameraman had to prove he could thread the camera, but the director didn't have to prove anything. All he had to do was to shout and beguile his actors. The silent directors wrote skeleton scenarios, cut the films, sometimes wrote the titles, supervised the lighting, possibly acted in the pictures, and in general ran a pretty tight ship with cast and crew. In an effort to head off the soaring popularity and bargaining power of their stars, the studios tried to publicize the directors, but the public was unfamiliar with their task and never responded with much enthusiasm. Only D. W. Griffith and Cecil B. DeMille made reputations for themselves that had demonstrable boxoffice appeal during the silent era. In 1925 Paramount Pictures announced that its policy was henceforth to hand all creative reins to the director, but 1925 was also the year MGM's twenty-six-year-old vice-president Irving Thalberg institutionalized the supervisor system. Supervisors—or producers, as they were soon called—were management personnel who nominally knew so much about pictures that they could plan, organize, and oversee the work of director, cast, and crew.

After the movies crashed the sound barrier, directors were forced into new absurdities. The numbered script was invented and directors told to shoot the script as numbered. Every movement and every position of the camera were marked by the production staff, usually the producer together with special "shooting script" rewriters. Changes were not permitted; directorial creation was discouraged, interpretation crushed. In 1949 Josef von Sternberg could still say, tongue-in-cheek, "My job is to transfer the script to the screen—intact. They want to see if I can make an actor walk across the set."

The director was told to make a master shot of a scene in its entirety, then to move the camera closer and film the whole thing over again in "twoshots," and, finally, to make "chokers," or close-ups of each character. As late as 1970, a Hollywood director's independence could be gauged by the number of twoshots and chokers his film had. The "name" director with some clout didn't have to move in if he felt he had what he wanted in the master, while the second-string director had to take "protection shots" of the principals in twoshots and close-ups. Since the film was cut by an editor independently of the director, the routine filmmaker's work was usually hacked up into more shots than the picture of his Big Time confrere.

But the daily footage of even a Cecil B. DeMille, a John Ford, or a William Wyler was screened by the studio boss, a ritual continued today. Lew Wasserman runs incoming Universal "dailies" or "rushes" at his home three or four nights a week, and Gordon Stulberg dives into a basement screening room before leaving Fox studios every evening.

"Although I like and respect the people concerned," Ronald Neame said while shooting *The Poseidon Adventure*, "I do find this practice a distraction. Mainly because I don't like shooting for 'rushes.' You can show off with 'rushes.' Then when the film comes out, when it's cut, perhaps it isn't very good. Conversely, you may be shooting a sequence that fits into a certain place. You want to shoot it in a certain way, and it may not necessarily be entertaining in rushes. Only the director, and sometimes the producer, know what it's all about. In a major studio, you have perhaps fifteen or twenty people who see your rushes every day, sometimes before you do, so out come a lot of remarks, made with good will but which, for the most part, have little bearing on the final production."

Francis Ford Coppola finds the practice unfair and silly. "Actors are instructed to 'play a role' in a film that is shot in shattered fragments and their performances don't jell until the editing is done, if then," he said during the filming of *Godfather II*.

Directors used to be rated, and the ratings confidentially circulated among production departments. "One director would be 'good for five or six pages a day,' another 'two and a half, if you're lucky,' " Joseph Mankiewicz reminisced during *Sleuth*. "Woody [W. S.] van Dyke was MGM's pride, and no matter what the schedule, he'd invariably wind up a week under. A lot of it couldn't be cut together, or wouldn't match, or Joan Crawford's right eye would be offscreen—and just as invariably, there'd be a week of retakes for every week he'd finished ahead." [1]

Mankiewicz wrote and directed *All About Eve* as a salaried employe, a "gun for hire," as he called it, and Twentieth Century–Fox

1. *Action*, Mar.–Apr. 1973.

was, in fact, the creator. He received no compensation from the musical version, *Applause*, or from television series based on his films *The Ghost and Mrs. Muir* and *Five Fingers*. "I know of no instance in which such incredible contractual usurpations have even been challenged," he said, observing that his Paramount writing contracts as far back as 1932 referred by name to television rights. "As studio contracts were then written, whether you were Bill Faulkner, Bob Sherwood, Joe Blow, or Mankiewicz, every conceivable right to what you created—in every conceivable medium, past, present, and yet to be invented—was, in every conceivable aspect, turned over to the studio."

Ironically, some of the best American films were made during the years when the studios were almighty. The conventional explanation is that the studio bosses ruled with iron fists but that they also knew how to let people work.

"Nowadays, 80 percent of a director's time is spent making deals and the remaining 20 percent making films," Billy Wilder has said. "In the thirties and forties that ratio was the reverse."

A newer and subtler view is that far from being shackled by rigid work conditions, certain directors of the Golden Era were stimulated by limits and managed to put a personal imprint on the assigned material. A measure of their talent is the *tension* between that talent and the assembly line. There are no Absolutes in Hollywood. The system is flexible enough to accommodate both formula screenfare and works of enduring value.

Hollywood moviemaking is also a nine-to-five livelihood for tens of thousands of people, and progress obviously translates differently than in enlightened amateurism or in countries where moviemaking is heavily subsidized. As in any American industry, the power in Hollywood is divided between management and unions. If producers, agents, directors, and stars decide *what* will be on the screens next Christmas, the unions decide *how*. Besides the shifts in economics, advances in equipment design—which, ironically, have not complicated but simplified moviemaking technology and brought it closer to enlightened amateur status—are working against the unions. Theoretically, however, they still control the industry from the screenwriter making the first ten-page synopsis to the "boothman" projecting the finished film in the neighborhood theater.

The Directors' Guild of America (DGA) represents 70 percent of all filmmakers in the United States, and is not totally the elitist association of Glamourland millionaires its $2,000 initiation fee and one-percent-of-annual-earnings-over-$10,000 membership fee might indicate. Founded in 1936, with King Vidor as its first president, the DGA also represents assistant directors and, in live TV and videotape, stage managers. Of its total roster of just over 4,000, some 2,500 members are feature-film and TV directors—the Hollywood contingent outstrips the East Coast wing three to two (there is a minuscule "Midwest" group). The remainder of the membership is made up of some 750 assistants and 700 stage managers (the latter mainly concentrated in New York).

In its collective bargaining with the Association of Motion Picture and Television Producers (AMPTP), the guild's thrust has for years been in creative rights. Without neglecting money matters, the DGA has scored on *auteurist* fronts since 1966, and directors are approaching the "final cut"—full artistic control of what ends up on the screen.

If a filmmaker riding a success wave can command half a million dollars or more plus percentages (to write-direct-produce *At Long Last Love*, Fox paid Peter Bogdanovich $600,000) a director with a few relative successes behind him gets from $120,000 to $200,000 per film. The moment he has a hit, his asking price doubles. Many of Hollywood's older "helmers" are wealthy and a few are millionaires, but most are saddled with alimony payments to first wives and with Beverly Hills real estate, which forces them to keep their nose to the grindstone. As long as they can find work, their guild sees to it that they can keep their swimming pools. The minimum *anyone* can earn directing a feature is $1,250 a week for a guaranteed ten weeks. Directors of "long form" television—series, anthologies, and Movies of the Week—get almost as much, while makers of two-hour TV specials are paid like feature-film directors.

Praise and blame for a film fall increasingly on the directors. When their pictures are successful, they now have a more equitable share of the profits, but the emergence of the director has not yet translated into a renaissance of the cinema or, more modestly, a royal flush of first-string movies that everybody wants to see. In 1972 *Variety* surveyed 100 films that had earned $6 million or better in American-Canadian rentals and found that less than a dozen filmmakers showed a consistently high rate of profit. "Too many directors of high repute send forth too many features of low revenue yield," the trade paper noted, adding that directors may be even less reliable at the boxoffice than the much-maligned performers.

"A startling number of the directors seem to ride a fiscal roller-coaster that for high-low contrasts far outdistances before-the-camera talent. It is not unusual for a director's follow-up to a hit to drop to less than 10 percent of the former film's rentals. While it is not surprising when this occurs to the less nameworthy filmmakers, it is startling to note the lack of commercial carryover for some of the most media-touted names now making pix."

Mike Nichols headed the list. After establishing himself as Broadway's top comedy stage director, Nichols hit it big with his screen debut, *Who's Afraid of Virginia Woolf?*, and followed with two more hits, *The Graduate* and *Carnal Knowledge*, although a top-grossing film, *Catch-22*, was nevertheless a deficit. The runner-up was George Roy Hill. His costly but top-grossing *Hawaii* was followed by two successive hits, *Thoroughly Modern Millie* and *Butch Cassidy and the Sundance Kid*, but *Slaughterhouse Five* was a dud. Franklin J. Schaffner was number three, with *Planet of the Apes* and *Patton* on the winning side and *Nicholas and Alexandra* as a loser.[2]

But, directors retort, they are only now really getting into the driver's seat. The creative rights of the contract signed in December 1973 and expiring in December 1977 even make James Aubrey's recutting of new pictures during his tenure as Metro boss illegal, and only from 1974 on can movies be said to be almost totally their makers' version. Only now must producers say in advance who decides what the final film will look like; only now is the "director's cut" mandatory; only now must the director participate in all decision making.

The producing company must submit a "deal memo," an advance memorandum designating the person with veto power over the film if this "final cut" authority is not granted the director. The designee cannot delegate this authority, which means a director can accept or reject an assignment up front because he does or does not trust the person selected to make the final cut.

Theoretically, the director has always had the right to a cut, but he didn't always get it. Now, this cut is mandatory, meaning that

2. *Variety*, Aug. 9, 1972. *Variety* named, in descending order, after Nichols, Hill, and Schaffner, Arthur Hiller, Stanley Kubrick, Arthur Penn, and Gene Saks as the top money-making directors.

once the last shot is in the can, the producer can no longer haul off the negative and do with it as he pleases.

The notion that exposed film has an innate value burned into it was first tested in court in 1966, when Otto Preminger and George Stevens sued over the insertion of commercials. Preminger lost when in a New York Supreme Court he challenged Screen Gems (Columbia's TV subsidiary) and ABC to show cause why they should be allowed to "degrade" *Anatomy of a Murder* with commercials, thereby damaging his reputation as a filmmaker. One month later, Stevens attacked NBC over *A Place in the Sun* in a Los Angeles court. His suit ended in a draw. The court refused to restrain the network from showing the film with commercials, but warned that blurbs should be inserted in such a way as not to adversely affect or "emasculate" the artistic and pictorial quality or destroy the mood. Seven years later, the AMPTP joined the DGA in petitioning the networks to grant directors the right to edit for commercials.

A key clause now prevents producers from undercutting the director's cut, another festering source of discontent in the past. While the director's cut is in progress, all other cuts are categorically excluded.

Instead of grievances being submitted to a joint committee of studio and DGA heads, new "instant" arbitration permits guild and management each to choose an arbiter and authorizes both designees to select a third, neutral arbitrator. A salient feature of this arbitration is the requirement that in assessing compensatory damages, the arbiters must take into account a given employer's previous violations of directors' creative rights. Darryl Zanuck, Sam Spiegel, or even Aubrey, with their penchant for fiddling with directors' efforts, couldn't *afford* to work in contemporary Hollywood.

A producer no longer howls, "The part's yours, kid" to a teenager on his casting couch. He doesn't order a fast rewrite of the script, choose locations, or have sets built or costumes designed without his director. And it isn't enough that he "consult" his director. With the 1973 pact, the director has moved from the traditionally consultative role to a "participatory" role. To further strengthen its hand, the DGA has infiltrated management by purchasing stock in all film and TV companies and networks signatory to contracts with directors. "Stocks will be purchased in amounts that will entitle the guild to obtain accurate corporate information and to assert all rights of stockholders," a DGA announcement said in October 1973. Armed with ten shares of MGM stock, the guild two months later sued Metro for diverting funds to its Grand Hotel in Las Vegas and demanded an account of all profits derived from dividends paid to MGM president Kirk Kerkorian.

Robert Aldrich, who was the chairman of the guild's negotiating committee, said after six months' negotiation with the AMPTP that the contract was "sensational" but also that it was "an extraordinary meeting of minds." The DGA likes to characterize the Creative Bill of Rights as anything but an "adversary agreement."

For all his independence, Aldrich has not made a crusade of having the final cut on his own films. "I put great store in two public previews, and I act on what I learn at them," he said during the editing of *The Longest Yard*. "It seems to me that the guy who's putting up two or three million dollars has a right to a say. And if you respect each other, what he has to say may be valuable. If a guy is making changes because he is on an ego trip, or working off some hangups, you're in trouble anyway and you're going to be picked to death whether you've got the final cut or not.

"The moguls today are probably as smart as the giants like Harry Cohn and Louis B. Mayer; they may even be better marketers. But they can't always communicate with the filmmakers in the same language. So now you've got a new breed in between that I call the *translators*. They translate to the mogul what it is you want to do and they translate to you what the mogul thinks you ought to do. The chances for communications to get fouled up are beautifully increased."

The director's pact has not pleased everybody, especially not the screenwriters, who are not ready to concede any *auteurist* supremacy to directors. As represented by the Writers' Guild of America (WGA), Hollywood's writers have developed into a sour lot, bickering over sizes of screen credits and mounting near-suicidal wars against the "hyphenates" in their own ranks—writers who are also producers and/or directors, especially in television.

The WGA has negotiated billing provisions that say the screenwriter must have billing of the same size as the largest of other nonperforming credits in an effort to counteract a proliferation of what writers call "presentational" or "possessive" credits. If the WGA has its way, no film will be *by* someone unless this person is also the screenwriter.

Not all director-writer relationships are open confrontations. Although most budgets don't include provisions for writers' salaries during shooting, Waldo Salt, for example, has stayed on through filming of *Midnight Cowboy* and *The Day of the Locust*. "The whole thing is done with John Schlesinger acting as slave master," Salt says. "I think he's a beautiful director. We do improvisations during a two-week rehearsal period. On *Midnight Cowboy*, for example, we went through the whole script, then threw the book away. Dustin Hoffman and Jon Voight then just played the content of the scenes and not specific lines."

By definition, the director "directs" through script, actors, cameraman, composer, and editor, fusing these elements and efforts into a single pattern with a point and central theme. "On the screen," deadpans Charlton Heston, "the director is practically the whole picture."

There is a world of difference between the way a script reads and the way it plays, between the way a line comes across in a master shot and in a close-up. Tone and climate of a production is set by the director, and one of his first concerns is for his professional family. Many feel their crews should be informed and feel part of a team, and many handpick their key crew members with as much care as their second-line players.

The key people in the crew—the cinematographer, gaffer (chief electrician), camera operator, sound recorder, and property master—tend to be veterans with many more years' experience than the director. They check him out to discover if he knows his business. They will sense the frightened. They need him to help kick their own fears and doubts and want to be assured he knows what *he* is doing.

"Many crew problems arise because of the twenty-five-year veteran who is still doing a minor job," Jerry Lewis has written. "He will always introduce himself: 'I've been in the business twenty-five years.' With those few words, the director is in trouble. The quarter-century vet is a critic and he'll be doing eight-hour critiques on the director's work. He is the guy who stands about thirty feet away, half in shadow, half in light, nodding, 'Tsk, tsk, tsk'. . . . It is vital to top this man on the psychological level." [3]

Teamwork is a state of mind, and most filmmakers remain pretty cynical about it. If for one reason or another a director is replaced,

3. Jerry Lewis, *The Total Film-Maker*. New York: Warner Paperback Library, 1973.

the crew will go on functioning on that film or another show. If the crew are fired they will have another job. The director may not.

Setside actions and reactions follow individual temperaments. A Robert Altman set is the locus of improvised anarchy and intuitive test patterns, a Franklin Schaffner picture in the making progresses in as orderly a fashion as a marine regiment, and a Billy Wilder film advances in a flow of insults, puns, and cajoling jokes. Altman has a menagerie of stock players and campfollowers with whom he lives after hours. Few stars have been at Alfred and Alma Hitchcock's home. Between setups, Vincente Minnelli walks around humming and wondering what his characters should think. Wilder's favorite setside seat is on top of a stepladder. Richard Brooks has a green towel dangling from his left hip pocket and refuses to give out synopses. Milos Forman refuses to give his actors the scripts. John Cassavetes has no script at all (and regularly runs over budget filming his actors' improvisations on his loose story lines). Like Altman, Bob Rafaelson, Hal Ashby, and Michelangelo Antonioni encourage freedom of interpretation from their actors, but Roman Polanski takes an autocratic approach.

Coming off Rafaelson's *The King of Marvin Gardens*, Ashby's *The Last Detail*, and Antonioni's *The Passenger*, Jack Nicholson found Polanski's authoritarian directing both unsettling and refreshing. "I saw immediately that I wasn't going to be able to do the kind of character work that I'd have done with another kind of director," Nicholson told reporters during *Chinatown*. "Anyway, I don't know if I'd like always to be working in the same style and exploring in the same way. I like it that Roman's got an idea of what he wants."

John Huston also knows what he wants, but he directs his actors as little as possible. "The more one directs," he says, "the more there is a tendency to monotony. If one is telling each person what to do, one ends up with a host of little replicas of oneself."

Directors engage their material with the full force of their sensibilities, and most agree that story and actors are the twin pillars of the whole edifice. "Eighty percent of a picture is writing," says Wilder; "the other twenty percent is the execution, such as having the camera on the right spot and being able to afford to have good actors in all parts." Maturer directors feel that the creative give and take comes early, ideally during the last script rewrite, when director and writer can kick around ideas and possibilities. They feel that each day's shooting narrows the options and freezes the creative magma a little more solidly. "The script is always a problem of the first importance because it is inevitably a disaster to go into a picture with a script which isn't right," says Schaffner.

Directors usually rehearse with actors and the writer "around the table" for days and sometimes weeks before starting shooting. The rehearsing can continue on the set, although here time is more expensive. Otto Preminger has trained himself to forget that time is money. "Some actors just need more time and more rehearsal and some don't," he said during *Hurry Sundown*. "Some actors who are basically picture personalities cannot rehearse. They become what they call stale." On *Some Like It Hot*, Wilder went up to fifty-nine takes with Marilyn Monroe. She got better with each take, but Tony Curtis often tired and played successively worse, which created fresh tension and blowups.

What the director calls an ideal actor is someone who can shade a line, who has timing, control, knows about the camera, and has a relationship with the camera. "An actor must have an awareness of the size of his gesture, his motion, in relation to the size that his image will be on the screen," Huston says.

Arthur Penn feels the most important thing a director can contribute to his actors is a climate of freedom, within the discipline of the story, to express and experience their parts. "I let it happen more or less improvisationally. It's not unusual, it's very much the American method, the Actor's Studio technique."

To work through the actors' intellectual comprehension of the material also reflects the decentralization of the production process. Actors have become producers—they have commitments of conflicting sorts—and it is no longer possible to prepare a script in great detail in a major studio and then call in contract actors, whose time the company controls completely, and make the film in accordance with preconceived plans. It has become essential to be more flexible, to adjust to conditions, both practical and esthetic.

No director would want blind obedience—actors, as William Wyler says, who report to work saying, "Okay, boss, what do you want me to do?"

To such actors, Wyler says, "You've read the script and you know what's in it, so *you* show *me*. I've got an idea, but maybe you've got a better one and I want to see it." With experienced actors, Huston doesn't even tell them where to stand during the blocking out of a scene. "Sometimes they wait to be told and I always try to get them to take the reins themselves. I say, 'Let's rehearse the scene, you show me.' I'd say four out of five times the actors—especially if they are very good actors—take over right away. I don't have to say a word. For example, working with George C. Scott on *The Bible*, I seldom even gave a clue of direction and he did exactly what I wanted without any of us ever saying a word, practically. Only occasionally I would have to ask him to move a bit to the left or the right. His approach to the scene would be so real and true that I couldn't add anything, except those mechanical camera directions. Not all actors are that good and some you have to work a lot with. Sometimes very good actors need a lot of direction, too, but if they are gifted and intelligent one is on the same wavelength anyway and one can talk in a kind of code. They catch what you want, use it, and it comes to you stronger, better, than you gave it to them, because they have digested it and are using their talents to put it into reality." [4]

"With some actors you have only to ask for more or less of a desired emotion," says Francis Ford Coppola. "On *The Godfather*, I literally told Marlon Brando to be 'more sad' and watched the extra lines appear on his forehead. Al Pacino is very insecure away from live theater and has to be approached through his totems. James Caan prefers little assignments to help him with a role. I try to reduce the tedium by giving my actors skits to work out during technical delays—charades that will get them deeper into their characterizations."

A powerful piece of the mosaic of filmmaking is the movie's sound track, its music. Although scoring comes after the editing, music is something directors—and producers—are paying increasing attention to. Film sound tracks account for more than half of all best-selling instrumental albums, and hit songs are effective advertising for films and often colossal moneymakers on their own.

Films have always had music. As long ago as 1908, obliging Camille Saint-Saëns is said to have whipped up some incidental music to a one-reeler, *L'Assassinat du Duc de Guise*, and movie music started in the orchestra pits of silent movie theaters with live musicians. The father of talking film music is Max Steiner, who came to Hollywood in 1929 and subsequently scored more than two

4. *Film Quarterly*, fall 1965.

hundred pictures, including *Gone with the Wind* and *Casablanca*. The present breed includes such composers as Henry Mancini, John Barry, Burt Bacharach, Paul McCartney, and Quincy Jones, men at home in jazz, rock, and pop rather than in the symphonically oriented scores of Maurice Jarre, Alex North, or Elmer Bernstein.

Spurning the large, thickly textured orchestra, these new movie composers nevertheless underscore the dramatic line, give "color" to the screen, and, as Stravinsky said, fill the emptiness of the screen. "A completed film score, by its very nature as a dramatic underscore, is just a series of music fragments put together in meaningless sequence," says Mancini.

Scoring is done under the explicit direction of the director. "It's not as bad as it sounds," says Bacharach. "Remember, the director has lived with the picture for a year." After seeing the film over and over again, sometimes aided at home by a Movieola machine, a composer works with a detailed synopsis of every action in every scene, each musical start and stop timed precisely: Begin music at 1 minute and 2 seconds as the door opens, surge to a crescendo at 1:06⅔, and stop at 1:10⅓ when the door shuts. To a movie composer, a stopwatch is more important than a piano."

"When I work on a score," says Mancini, "I want to get my own approach completely free from anyone else's influence. I don't want to talk to the director or the actors. I don't want to know anything but what is actually in the finished movie. All this business about going on location to 'soak up atmosphere' is ridiculous. I rarely even read the script because often what's on paper doesn't make it to the screen. I look at the film, no more than four or five times. While I'm looking, I get the scenes, the story, the mood. Then I go home and work on the score."

The pressure is nevertheless on to compose at least one hit song or a tune that is "exploitable." "Composers are caught between trying for a hit and a score that should be dramatic," says André Previn. "All of us love to write songs, but I object to the shoehorning in of a pop song where it has no place." Mancini feels it is impossible to separate music for the movies from pop music and that combining the two can be very rewarding for a composer.

A director, John Ford repeatedly told interviewers and young would-be filmmakers, should know in advance what is and isn't possible. A director must be aware of each staff member's operation and functions and in general be knowledgeable about sound, optics, cold readings, processing, effects, insurance, music scoring, dubbing, editing, script steplines, wardrobe, makeup, color, sets, design, Stanislavski, and his own homework. What he tries to guard against in particular is seeping deterioration and his own giving in to second, third, and fourth choices. Every director knows what it means when the script demands a jeep, but none is available immediately so it becomes a taxi. Budget pressures tend to make filmmaking a nightmare of little compromises.

"With every film I find out a little more about myself," said Steven Spielberg just before starting *Jaws*. "Shooting a movie is like shooting unguided missiles: You hope it lands where you want it to land."

But what really makes the director sweat during filming is his own vulnerability to disease. A particular curse of modern film financing is the need to insure not only stars against falling off horses and the negative against airplane hijackings, but the production itself. Because backers have lost money on pictures that were never finished, any budget now includes upward of $50,000 in premiums on so-called completion bonds and a host of other insurances. Lloyd's of London is the principal insurer of films, although there are others in the field, and to figure its premiums it runs computer charts of all leading stars and directors. Since all off-camera personnel can be replaced, only stars can cause a film to be totally canceled and have themselves declared uninsured, which explains why old directors can continue to work and old actors cannot be cast in starring roles (at seventy-eight, Charles Chaplin could make *The Countess from Hong Kong* as a director with a walk-on; as leading man in every shot he would have been uninsurable).[5] To avoid "graylisting" on Lloyd's computer sheets, directors will have themselves carried up mountains on stretchers, and shot full of antibiotics at the least provocation, and will hire setside physicians rather than add two days to a forty-day schedule.

One of the stickier problems of contemporary film financing lies here. Not only do private investors want to be sure the project they are pouring money into will eventually emerge as a film, studios also want to be sure the budget agreed upon before shooting is also "the bottom line." Twentieth Century–Fox executives have nothing

5. Stanley Kramer had great difficulty insuring *Guess Who's Coming to Dinner* because of the poor health record of sixty-year-old Spencer Tracy. The picture came in "just under the wire," as cynics said, since Tracy died before it was even released.

against the admittedly stiff $6 million budget for Peter Bog-
danovich's *At Long Last Love*, if they—and, ultimately more important, their bank creditors—can be sure there will be no surprises
enroute, that the musical will be no bottomless pit, but indeed
something that will cost $6 million. Insurance companies will guar-
antee such budgets, but their involvement means they will want to
have the power to step in to protect themselves if things go wrong.
The present rule of thumb is that if a filmmaker falls more than
four days behind schedule, he is in trouble. Another day or two
and the completion guarantor may step in and, reluctantly, halt
production and impose a replacement director.

Traditionally, the best directing is the least conspicuous. Esthetics change constantly, however, forcing corresponding upheavals in
style and concepts. The Aquarian Age with its intense, visionary
trading on an amplified "now" demanded tell-it-like-it-is realism. A
few years later, entertainment for entertainment's sake brought demands for glare and shine. This trend has also brought about a
modest renaissance in studio filming.

The stages filmmakers drifted back to were not the same old pad-
ded barns they fled in the 1960s. "Flying wall" sets are now increasingly appealing to directors who have experimented with in-
tractable shooting in real apartments. Contemporary studios are
increasingly made according to the plug-in principle—all facilities
and technologies are "modular," i.e., any part of the studio is used
as a standard to which the rest is proportioned.

Movies that are not shooting on stages are practically all Cinemobile operations in one form or another. The development of self-
contained mobile production units requiring less help has fostered a
new look in filmmaking. Equipment and "hardware" are radically
different in design and adaptability from the technical apparatus of
even a few years ago. The cameraman's tyranny has been reduced
by advances in camera and film stock technology. Overall, technical
advances (see Chapter 14) have made the mechanics of moviemaking far less forbidding than during the Golden Era.

8

Visceral Impact

THE MEDIUM *has* become a large hunk of the message, and nowhere are input and feedback of the "visual society" as dramatic as in that mother medium of the century, the cinema. Technology moves, transforms, and amplifies. It also widens our senses, our ability to see and hear and even that synthesizing sense, the ability to think.

Today's movies are visual feasts—tensile looks and emotional colorings—and new moviegoers respond to camera work. They float with Vilmos Zsigmond's evanescent sepia photography in *McCabe and Mrs. Miller*, tense up with his lush but portending riverscapes in *Deliverance*, and glide through an absurd America on his endless ribbons of highway in *The Sugarland Express*. *Easy Rider*, *Five Easy Pieces*, *Paper Moon*, and *Shampoo* owe a lot of their sweep to Laszlo Kovacs, just as *Butch Cassidy and the Sundance Kid* and *The Day of the Locust* owe a lot of their visual command to Conrad Hall's overexposed and desaturated color photography. Today a film's cameraman is "cast" with almost as much deference as its performers. The premium is on the person whose *seeing* is expressed with a little more originality, with better composition or planning or quicker responses, the person who shoots at that one moment when everything comes together, the person who explores new ideas and gives tone and vitality to the screen. The cameraman—or cinematographer or director of photography—plays a starring role diametrically opposite to the one assigned him in classical Hollywood. Then, the less conspicuous his imprint the better. Today, the *look* of a film is part of its awareness and of the visceral experience of seeing it.

Contemporary cameramen enjoy a greater range of materials and are permitted a greater amount of artistry than before, even though fast schedules may sometimes cramp their style. Today equipment, film stock, and laboratory methods are undergoing a worldwide standardization, and national "schools" of cinematography are tending to disappear in the general media blur. The current trend is toward desaturation in color through over- and underexposure, toward faster film stocks and wider lenses, allowing for more sensuous surfaces and an up-close kind of filmmaking that, at its best, translates into less linear, more seductive and urgent movies. At its worst, it becomes the visual equivalent of rock music smeared on the sound track like body paint, slow-motion sunflare clichés.

The cameraman is the newest cult figure.

The extent of the cinematographer's contribution to the making of a film varies from one picture to another. Most of the time it is a collaboration between the director and the cameraman; but even this is inconsistent, depending on the director's attitude, capability, and personality.

"You can't do good photography with a director who doesn't know how to tell a story with your camera," says Zsigmond ("Ziggy" to most of Hollywood).

Senior cameramen are still at work, but newer men *are* taking over local 659, for fifty years the most tightly closed of the closed-shop International Alliance of Theatrical and Stage Employes (IA) unions. James Wong Howe, who shot his first movie at Paramount in 1923, was still at it in 1974, photographing Barbra Steisand in *Funny Lady,* but the two hundred cameramen aged sixty and over who dominated local 659 in the mid-1960s have finally faded out, and with them the more abstruse union rules. A full-fledged Group One cameraman can *almost* operate his own camera now—"almost" meaning some of the time but not all the time.

"Who has ever heard of a violin operator?" Kovacs can say now. Only a few years ago, someone would have been watching to assure that union rules weren't broken, to file reports and complaints if a Group One cinematographer felt compelled to operate his own camera.

The ascension of Hollywood's four leading cameramen—Conrad ("Connie") Hall, Haskell Wexler, Kovacs, and Zsigmond—has been one long obstacle course over archaic union rules. Hall and Wexler were caught in drawn-out jurisdictional battles between the IA and Hollywood's other union combine, the National Association of Broadcast Engineers and Technicians (NABET). Kovacs had *Getting Straight, Five Easy Pieces, The Last Movie,* and *Alex in Wonderland* behind him before he got to shoot interiors on a major studio stage. (*Marriage of a Young Stockbroker,* at Fox, which had rejected him for *M*A*S*H.*)

Arriving in the United States from his native Hungary together with Zsigmond in 1957, Kovacs made his way to Los Angeles via Seattle, where he worked in a television station lab. The TV crews in Seattle had trouble pronouncing his name, so he became Leslie Kovacs. When he became a naturalized citizen in 1963, he legally assumed the name Leslie, which had been on the credits of all his early films. It was Peter Bogdanovich who insisted that he revert to Laszlo for *Targets,* possibly to continue the early New Wave in-joke that had Jean-Paul Belmondo play a character named Lazslo Kovacs in various Claude Chabrol and Jean-Luc Godard movies.

In L.A., Kovacs worked for several years in the microfilm photo lab of a title insurance company, but "the two green Hungarians," Kovacs and Ziggy, were available for any and all bootleg and low-budget film assignments, often as the complete crew.

Kovacs' first feature film as a cameraman was *Mark of the Gun,* a $10,000 black-and-white western for which he and several others pooled their savings. The film was never sold or released, but it did serve as an audition for director Richard Rush, who needed and found a good and inexpensive cinematographer for *A Man Called Dagger,* a picture which, in turn, provided Kovacs with the credit needed to begin filming commercials with "an incredible genius maniac" named Lee Lacy, a pioneer in the use of long-lense-rack-focus photography.

Kovacs was back with Richard Rush at AIP, filming *Hell's Angels on Wheels* in quasi-TV commercial style, with preview flash cuts of upcoming scenes, a device later used in *Easy Rider.* Rush and Kovacs also sought to develop the shallow-rack-focus technique for storytelling purposes, "rationing," as they said, the flow of visual information to the viewers' eyes through critical focusing between planes of action within the frame, i.e., editing in the camera by staging scenes in the depth of the frame, as Gregg Toland did in *Citizen Kane* and in the William Wyler classics. They experimented in the AIP drug and bike flicks *Psych-Out* and *The Savage Seven*, and by the time Kovacs had photographed *Easy Rider*, all this was suddenly a new, "spaced out" style.

Kovacs is rather modest about his own contribution and says the work in the 1960s of Connie Hall, William Fraker, and Wexler is what has influenced style in filmmaking everywhere.

Hall, who says he desperately misses black and white—he filmed such late b&w pictures as Richard Brooks's *In Cold Blood* (1967) and says *Fat City*, which he photographed for John Huston, would have been better in black and white—began experimenting with overexposure in color on *Tell Them Willie Boy Is Here* and continued on *Butch Cassidy and the Sundance Kid*.

"The trouble with overexposing is that it can look *too* beautiful and a little bit unreal." Hall began desaturating colors on *Hell in the Pacific*, using filters in the camera and in the subsequent laboratory process to take the color out.

"There is too much use of color in color filming," he says, echoing a sentiment shared by Zsigmond, who uses a lot of soft lighting and overexposure to tone down reds, blues, and other "sickly colors" and in general leans toward impressionism in screen artistry. Zsigmond also feels that hand-held camera work—which is useful for producing a screen effect of urgency and nervousness (tracking a fleeing criminal, for example)—has been overdone. "The Panaflex is a lightweight camera, but it still tires you when you hand-hold it for rehearsal after rehearsal and take after take," he says. "I think it's best to put the camera on a tripod. In my opinion, you should use the hand-held camera only when it adds to the excitement of the shot."

Fraker, a second-generation Hollywood workhorse (his father was a studio still photographer) has also worked at the reduction of colors and is perhaps at his best outdoors, in striking uses of light, dust clouds, and rain, and in submerging and then unifying disparate elements of landscapes. Fraker went to USC film school as a classmate of Hall and with *Games* became a full-fledged cinematographer (he was Hall's operator on *The Professionals*). After *Rosemary's Baby*, he filmed such open-air bravura pieces as *Bullit* and *Paint Your Wagon* before trying his hand at directing with the Lee Marvin starrer, *Monte Walsh*, a less than successful western followed by an equally drooping Hitchcock imitation (photographed by Kovacs), *A Reflection of Fear*. James Wong Howe and Karl

Freund are a couple of other Hollywood cameramen who have dabbled in direction before returning to cinematography.

The "brutal honesty" technique owes much of its big-screen acceptance to Haskell Wexler, like Hall an independently wealthy dabbler in documentaries who established himself as a cameraman with *America, America, The Loved One,* and *Who's Afraid of Virginia Woolf?* Wexler made his color debut on *In The Heat of the Night* and, in deference to the subject, desaturated the colors to create a realistic "black and white color." On his next film, *The Thomas Crown Affair,* he went the other way and made the colors rich and vivid, in keeping with Steve McQueen's lavish on-screen life.

In 1968 Wexler coproduced, wrote, directed, and filmed *Medium Cool,* the story of a news cameraman's growing sense of responsibility toward the injustices he photographs. Shot during the Democratic convention in Chicago (at one point Wexler was himself teargassed), *Medium Cool* used no sets and virtually no lighting, and all sound was authentic, with practically no post-dubbing. The film was a new kind of staccato moviemaking, full of devastating cityscapes, foul-mouthed close-ups, and hand-held riots. With various results, this elliptical cinema, with its emphasis on complicity and laconic and at the same time disturbing immediacy, is being used the world over, with France's Claude Lelouch—also his own cameraman—and Constantin Costa-Gavras the most famous practitioners of this shorthand narrative style.

Radicalized by the experience, Wexler went to South America and directed and filmed *Brazil, A Report on Torture.* He continued his double life as cameraman (on *Trial of the Catonsville Nine* and *American Graffiti,* on which his credit reads "visual consultant") and as producer-cinematographer (maker of commercials for Schlitz, Ford, Volkswagen, Kool-Aid, and Coca Cola). Francis Ford Coppola hired him to photograph *The Conversation,* then replaced him with Bill Butler. In *Action,* Coppola said he fired Wexler because "when the rushes came in I just didn't feel he was getting what I wanted on the screen." [1] In a *New York Times* interview, Wexler remembered it a little differently, saying his firing was an excuse Coppola needed "to break the picture for three weeks or so in order to do the preparation he had neglected . . . and get himself together." [2]

1. *Action,* May–June, 1973.
2. *New York Times,* Aug. 12, 1973.

Like Zsigmond, Wexler feels the color photography of tomorrow will be impressionistic. "The best light for most color effects is transient, either at sunrise or at sunset," he says, "but if a director doesn't plan his exteriors with that in mind, the film ends up being photographed in the bleaching light of midday. In Hollywood, we've got harsh, smoggy sunlight to deal with most of the time."

On *Theives Like Us*, Robert Altman and cameraman Jean Boffety (this Frenchman replaced Zsigmond because of conflict of schedules), tried to shoot exteriors only at dawn and at dusk to capture with maximum intensity the natural beauty of Tennessee and Alabama, but ran into union rules forbidding a split-up of the crew's work day (unless the production was willing to pay triple time after 1:00 P.M.).

The new cinematographers work increasingly with lightweight equipment but are still complaining about unwieldy "dinosaur" sound cameras. "For the future, we need a research and development program that will drastically change the design of cameras," says Kovacs. "It took the Mitchell Corporation thirty years to come up with a reflex camera. The engineers who are designing cameras don't understand our problems. We're still working with cameras that weigh eighty to one hundred pounds, when we need a lightweight silent hand-held one."

9

Deeper into Money

WITH THE EXCEPTION of architects designing soaring rhetoric on Park Avenue or spreading permissiveness over suburban arts centers, filmmaking remains the most expensive of the arts. Money, inevitably, talks.

Financing and distribution—making a picture and getting it to market—are the twin pillars of the whole edifice, and the two are irrevocably entwined. It is not realistic to finance the production of movies alone, and it is not financially practical only to distribute them. Distribution is a terribly expensive business and really only makes sense on a global scale.

Nationalities—and nationalism—are tricky in films. Audiences and critics may talk about an American or an Italian film, but a good hunk of the world production has nothing to do with little flags on the Cannes Croisette. Even so, the movies are the first of the arts—ahead of TV and literature—to live in the global village. Since the early 1960s big movies have flown, at best, flags of convenience while, ironically, progressive and "radical" films have been puritanically nationalistic.

Just as it is ludicrous to call Norman Jewison and Arthur Hiller Canadian filmmakers (their passports may be, but *Jesus Christ Superstar* and *Plaza Suite* are not Canadian points of view), it is vain to assess the nationalities of most big (a budget of more than $5 million) films made today. Perhaps few people would hesitate to call *Tora! Tora! Tora!* (a film about Pearl Harbor) American, although half of it was directed by Akira Kurosawa (or his assistants, since he reportedly went quite mad during filming), but what about *Dr. Zhivago* or *Nicholas and Alexandra*? Are they Spanish (where they were made), Russian (their source material), British and American (their casts, directors David Lean and Franklin Schaffner), or American (their money)? What is the nationality of *The Little Prince*?

With *Zabriskie Point* Michelangelo Antonioni gave in to his own demons of saying something about America, and with *The Touch* Ingmar Bergman made it into that *cinéma apatride* of multinational and multilingual sound track, cast, and finances that Luis Buñuel, Luchino Visconti, and others have practiced for years, leaving Federico Fellini about the only director in the international pantheon never to have labored outside his own idiom and national conscience.

The Hollywood majors are unique world powers who were "multinationals" when oil was a series of unconnected cottage industries for Texans, Venezuelans, and a few Lawrences of Arabia. If François Truffaut wants to have *Day for Night* seen not only in Tokyo and Rio de Janeiro but also in Osaka and Myazaki, Recife and Belo Horizonte, his film becomes a UA or a Warner release. A Carlo Ponti or Dino de Laurentis usually retains Italy for himself while selling other "territories" to a major. This is what the annual Cannes festival is all about—trading off hemispheres, or, if worst comes to worst, individual countries when the majors won't buy. A Danish producer or Cekoslovensko Filmexport with a competing entry will try to make its film a Fox or a Warner's release—indeed hundreds of pictures, some only half finished, are brought to Cannes every year to be shown to moneylenders for additional financing. It is only when the producers cannot raise the interest of Columbia, Fox, Paramount, Warner's, and/or UA that they begin to sell piecemeal—French-speaking territories to a Parisian distributor, Uruguayan rights to a Montevideo outfit, etc.

Movies are made with millions of dollars, but the return comes back in hundreds of millions of cents, and the distribution fee is not just the payment for marketing, but a reward for taking the risks of handling a film. "When a picture is a success, that reward is too high; and when it is a disaster, it is too low," *The Economist*'s David Gordon has said. "The only way distributors can survive is by setting the super-profits of one production against the super-losses of another and the nothing profits of the average picture." [1]

This globe-girdling presence (UA is not only an Italian distributor but also an Italian producing company) demands such cash outlays that even American majors have been forced to pool their resources. In 1970 Paramount and Universal formed Cinema International Corporation (CIC) in Amsterdam (Holland was considered to have the healthiest tax climate and most lenient labor laws in Europe for this "offshore" enterprise). There is periodic talk of similar combines of Fox and Warner's, or even a joint Warner's-Fox-Columbia releasing company, but old habits so far have scuttled such ideas.

Distributors and theater owners don't see eye to eye on the figures, but roughly sixty cents of each dollar clunked down at the boxoffice stays right there. Sixty percent is pretty stiff in most retailing, but mortgage payments, depreciation, and advertising are uncommonly high for movie houses, since they thrive best in choice locations and since ads on the entertainment page are always higher than in any other newspaper section. Together with staff salaries, rent and advertising account for 55 percent of a theater's expenditures. The rental of the film itself represents another 36 percent, leaving a profit margin of less than 10 percent.

Very roughly, the majors each spend $10 million in North America (moviewise, Canada has always been part of the "domestic" scene) and $10 million in the rest of the world every year to maintain sales offices. The returns are proportionate.[2] Foreign earnings account for about half of the total, and improvements abroad usually offset drops in domestic rentals and vice versa (musicals don't travel well, while other genres can take on astonishing lives in unsuspected areas—Hal Ashby's *Harold and Maude* played two years in Paris before it became a French stage play).

Like a national airline and a seat in the United Nations, films are part of most countries' psychic paraphernalia. *All* governments spend public funds on the prestige that filmmaking represents—in inverse proportion, it seems, to the national cinema's importance.

1. *Sight and Sound*, autumn 1973.
2. In descending order, the ten top countries for American movies are, according to Motion Picture Export Association figures: Italy, West Germany, Britain, France, Japan, Australia, South Africa, Brazil, Spain, and Mexico.

The lesser the significance, the heavier the subsidies and the money spent on the annual information booth at the Cannes Carlton. In Brazil, for example, foreign movies are taxed a whopping 40 percent and the local industry is further protected by compulsory exhibition of local films eighty-four days of the year (regardless of the quality). Yet the only significant work to come out of Brazil has been of the subversive and militant variety banned at home by the Brazilian government. There are "name" directors in Canada, Czechoslovakia, Germany, and the Ivory Coast whose government-financed films have never earned a penny, even in their homelands, and who travel on public expense to festivals in Tehran, Berlin, Carthage, and Plata del Mar to denounce the Philistines of film commerce while charging screening rooms to their host country or their national delegation in the hope that imperialist distributors will see their work and assure their place among the immortals of film.

Few people in production are happy with the system. Of the forty cents going back to the distributor from the theater, only fifteen cents are available for the negative cost of the film and the rest is swallowed up in overheads and profits.

Loyalties on both sides are in proportion to the most recent hit or miss. Coppola is not likely to bitch about the release Paramount gave *The Godfather*, nor is Universal likely to hold *American Graffiti* against George Lucas. Besides, there is no real alternative. Financing a film without a distribution deal is suicide, and the present love-hate relationship is likely to continue.

"I don't think anybody in the position of creating films is totally happy with the distributor—it's a natural rivalry—but in actuality, the distributor is usually competent and able and I have learned the hard way that I can't direct a film and then try to distribute it myself," says Stanley Kramer. "I think it was Sam Goldwyn who said, 'If I've got a smash, you can't hurt me and if I've got a failure, you can't help me.'" Strong-willed directors have usually learned the hard way. Dissatisfied with the way MGM handled *Brewster McCloud* and the way Warner's handled *McCabe and Mrs. Miller*, Robert Altman financed *Images* himself, with the help of Hemdale, a young British company. "The whole experience was not very pleasant," Altman said a year later. "I now think it's probably a mistake not to have a distributor involved in a film from the time you enter production. Columbia didn't even know until two months beforehand that they were going to handle *Images*, so they didn't have much time to formulate advertising and marketing."

"The great danger of total independent financing is that without a studio behind you from the start, you are taking the risk, the very high risk, that the major won't be interested in distributing your film once you finish it," says Al Ruddy, producer of *The Godfather*. "There are consistently fifty or more feature-length films sitting on lab shelves that you can pick up for lab fees. The producers went their own way and then couldn't get distribution. Since filmmaking is such a high-risk business to begin with, why add more risks?"

Since only 15 percent of the odd $3 billion that American-distributed pictures gross around the world goes back into production, it means the industry has slightly under $500 million in revolving funds to reinvest each year. That is about the amount the market can support, and outside financing is constantly being sought.

If Mattel, General Foods, Reader's Digest, and Fabergé supposedly know what they are getting into (CBS and ABC obviously didn't, since they pulled out after losing tens of millions of dollars each), outside money is usually raised on a false note. The most common—and ultimately the most demeaning—is the tax write-off.

An individual or a corporation enjoying windfall earnings, which must be invested if the Internal Revenue Service isn't to get its hands on them, is invited to join in a syndicate to produce a film. The most convincing part of the producer's argument is usually that if worst comes to worst and the film is a flop, the investment can be treated as a tax write-off.

"I'm against this method because you aren't raising capital with the property, the ingredients, the budget, and your professional approach," says producer Arnold Orgolini, who has administered shopping center and rock music money invested in films. "The professional approach is to show your potential backers your safeguards for bringing the picture in, your guarantees, the kind of people you have in mind, their track records."

Also, the IRS is tightening its tax laws to prevent a $100,000-a-year dentist, for example, from writing off $10,000 invested in a film—or any other activity not directly related to dentistry.

Most venture capital is found closer to home. Cinemobile's founding father, Fouad Said, has raised production capital from Taft Broadcasting, Hemdale of London, and UA Theaters, all entertainment-related companies, and the Hollywood trade press constantly announces new corporation formations to bring in "resourceful venture capital from nontraditional sources," even if filmmaking appears pretty far down the list of favorites for risk capitalists.[3]

What had always caused frustration and ill-will inside the industry and made investors, small and big, shy away is the film business's Byzantine bookkeeping and financial secrecy.

"It makes you laugh perhaps," says Rod Steiger, "but the major problem facing big-name actors is getting paid. We're being had. We all know it, but we don't dare speak about it."

What makes Steiger mad is the practice of no longer paying stars but having them "participate" in their films' financial fortunes. It has been the solution to both inflation of movie star salaries and to so-called independent filmmaking. Steiger and others are the first to admit that star salaries had been getting out of hand. Participation, at least in principle, *should* mean greater creative freedom. But, he says, participation implies honest bookkeeping.

"Too many producers are cheating performers," says Steiger. "Contracts basically don't mean anything, because the person for whom you're working calculates how long it's going to take you before you can get him into court. Meantime, he uses your money, earning 6 to 10 percent interests for three, four years. Then he waits until you get up on the court calendar. By that time you're half spastic, and in the last minute he offers you an out-of-court settlement. What's really crazy is that you accept this—gratefully, thinking it's better than nothing."

In 1972 Steiger had yet to collect his first dollar on *The Pawnbroker*, which he did for 2 percent of the gross and $25,000 up front and which won him an Oscar nomination in 1965. He refused to be "shredded" and eventually won a $50,000 judgment, which he was obliged to share with fellow plaintiff Sidney Lumet, the director, who had also worked on deferment. By the time the ruling was handed down, Commonwealth United, the producing company, was in bankruptcy.

Steiger has suggested that the Screen Actors' Guild (SAG) create a protection service for its members. This unit, composed of accountants, would enforce collection of percentages and force talent

3. According to *Business Week* (Nov. 3, 1973), "venture investors" prefer medical products, communications equipment, service industries, and environmental controls before "leisure companies."

agents to negotiate contracts providing for continuous payments, access to books to insure an honest count, and a rising scale of penalties for offending producers. Although actual court cases are rare, the SAG is involved in scores of labor arbitrations every year on behalf of its members.

Any producer feeling himself pointed at by Steiger will turn around and point a finger at the distributors, who, in turn, will point to the theater owners. To Steiger it is called "cheating the actor," to the producer it's "yo-yo bookkeeping," and to the major distributor it's exhibitor "underreporting."

Part of the industry's new maturity is its newly adopted uniform accounting methods. Recommended by the American Institute of Certified Public Accountants and scheduled to go into effect in 1975, the new guidelines will eliminate such whimsical practices as Columbia's "contract method" of reporting the income of a TV sale the moment the contract is signed even though payment is received later, MCA's reporting of TV profits even before the film is aired, or MGM's "deferral method" of taking its profits evenly over the entire period of license prior to network airing. Also restricted under the new CPA ruling is the practice of capitalizing interest on cash borrowed to make a film. "We had quite a session on that point, but the majority determined that it was not proper to use interest on bank loans as a production cost because films are an inventory item, not a long-term asset," said Seymour Bohrer, the New York accountant who captained a nine-man CPA team that wrote the guidelines. In 1958 William Wyler filed suit against Samuel Goldwyn for adding the director's participation to the negative cost of *The Best Years of Our Lives*, which meant that the more money the picture made the higher the break-even point and the less the actual percentages of its earnings going to Wyler. Goldwyn settled out of court in 1962, sixteen years after the picture was made.

The Motion Picture Producers' Association is secretive when it comes to any in-depth figures, and annual fiscal reports by the majors are even chided by *Variety* for lacking financial "visibility." Such a potential landmark development as Ely Landau's movies-by-subscription American Film Theater was shrouded in mystery even after its success was assured. It was a slip-of-the-tongue at an Allied Artists stockholders' meeting that revealed that the $13 million price tag of *Papillon* represented six times the net worth of the entire company.

The break-even point is what separates producer and distributor. Unless a film is such a runaway smash hit that the money pouring in cannot possibly be hidden, the participating producer, director, and/or on-screen talent have only the distributor's word for it that the picture has not yet broken even.

From the beginning, *everything* is charged against the picture. If Fox becomes the financing distributor of *Winner Take All*, the project is given a production number and Fox employes will charge everything from office space and xeroxing to car rentals and recording tapes to that number. If the New York publicity chief has an urgent question to ask his West Coast confrere, he must charge the long-distance call to *Winner Take All*, or some other film-in-production he finds appropriate. All this is called "overhead," and it adds up to as much as 30 percent of the below-the-line budget, i.e., the production cost excluding the cast. In order to attract independents, studios lower the overhead they charge outsiders to between 15 and 25 percent.

A typical "independent" deal means Fox will finance the independent producer's picture with the proviso that he use Fox facilities—offices, stages, equipment, lab, editing rooms, and scoring and mixing stages—and, of course, that the picture becomes a Fox release. Below-the-line costs escalate with such obvious expenses as period costuming, set construction, mass scenes, and not-easy-to-control (and therefore time-consuming) street exteriors. But how much does it cost to make a movie?

Shooting *The Dark Tower* at Warner's in the fall of 1973, Arthur Penn's daily cost was $22,000. Cinemobile, however, will furnish union crew and equipment at between $900 and $1,500 a day, meaning a thrifty producer can shoot a modestly budgeted film, on location, for about $3,000 a day, below the line.

To release a picture *is* expensive. There are about 10,000 permanent four-wall cinemas and 4,500 drive-in theaters in the United States, employing just under 200,000 people full-time. There are about 700 circuits, each with four or more theaters, operating some 55 percent of the total houses. More than 60 percent of all domestic earnings come from 1,000 key-run bookings. New York City alone represents 15 percent of the total take, and half of all rentals come from just six cities: New York, Los Angeles, San Francisco, Philadelphia, Chicago, and Boston. The advantage of the majors over the small independent distributor is the ability to book, sight unseen, into these key markets and to get these bookings in advance.

The price is stiff. Advertising and media costs in New York are such that some films never have a New York premiere.

"Economically, it's almost prohibitive," says Avco Embassy Pictures vice-president D. J. Edele. In 1974 a line of advertising in the *New York Times*' Sunday entertainment section reached $4.98, meaning that a full-page ad cost $11,962. Expenditures of $40,000 to $50,000 in pre-opening and first-week advertising and publicity are not uncommon. Paramount poured $85,000 into pre-opening and first-week advertising for *Jonathan Livingston Seagull*, and the picture grossed less than $10,000 in its first week and was down to half that amount by the fourth week. Avco Embassy mounted a $130,000 campaign for *The Day of the Dolphin*.

The going is even rougher on foreign films because theater owners don't participate in the advertising expenses. "We pay advertising one hundred percent," says Fox's John Friedkin, adding that despite rave reviews and a healthy and long New York run, Fox wound up with less than $200,000 in profits from Luis Buñuel's 1972 smash hit *The Discreet Charm of the Bourgeoisie*. "What's more," says Edele, "New York opening costs set the pace for those in Los Angeles and Chicago."

A New York premiere is practically essential for most movies, foreign and domestic, which require critical endorsement to launch a national campaign. Several minimajors, however, have deserted Gotham—Cinerama successfully skirted the New York opening on *Walking Tall, Arnold,* and *W.* Excluding key cities, a nationwide advertising campaign can be mounted for what it costs to open in midtown Manhattan.

Besides the obvious expense of prints and advertising, maintaining offices and staff across the United States and around the world to service this complex operation adds 60 percent to a film's cost. If *Winner Take All* costs $2 million to make, it has to bring the distributor $3.2 million in order to break even. But sixty cents of the box-office dollar stays with the theater, so the participating producer and/or talent will not see a penny until *Winner Take All* has grossed $5,120,000, or, as we said earlier, 2.7 or 2.8 times its cost.

The shoe *can* almost be on the other foot. It is not economically practical to have the distribution pipeline dry up, and the majors constantly seek independent films to release. If a producer has raised production financing himself, he may be in a position to negotiate a "gross deal," which will have him participate in whatever percentages he has negotiated for from the first dollar returned to the distributor. The gross deal has the distributor pay for prints and advertising—normally 200 prints and a publicity campaign costing between $250,000 and $500,000. The advantage to the producer is that the distributor is also risking something and therefore may push harder to recoup his investment. But, again, the independent producer has only the major's word for it that his picture has, or has not, reached break-even. The producer cannot stand in lobbies in a couple of thousand theaters and count ticket buyers. Nor can the distributor.

Which side cheats most? The majors accuse the theatermen of "underreporting," and the exhibitors complain about inflexible terms that include top rentals for second-rate movies, fixed minimum runs, and high guarantees (sometimes demanded even before a frame of film is exposed). High on the list of theater-owned complaints is the distributors' "whim of iron." Playdates are switched on a moment's notice and frequently an exhibitor doesn't know what he will be playing on his circuit three days in advance. Also irksome to theatermen is the disappearence of a sliding scale which meant that the more a picture grossed the more the distributor got, but the longer the picture ran the higher the exhibitor's percentage. Now distributors insist on "firm terms," with a scale of 60, 50, 40 percent respectively for each week of a three-week run, no matter how much—or little—a picture grosses. Theatermen's loudest howls are over guaranteed advances they have to come up with in order to get the highly touted big pictures. They have never cottoned to the idea that they should share the risk with distributors, and the bigger circuits have traditionally withheld playdates as their ultimate bargaining weapon. With the spreading of "four-walling"—where distributors simply rent a theater at a fixed weekly price—theater owners are increasingly seeking terms allowing some form of refunding on failures such as The Great Gatsby, for which Loews Theaters paid $1 million in advance for New York City, only to lose money every week during its six-week exclusive run.

Underreporting, or "skimming," is a touchy subject. When UA's general counsel Gerald Phillips addressed the 1973 convention of the National Association of Theater Owners (NATO) and said there would be few customers indeed if a distributor were to refuse films to all exhibitors suspected of skimming, his words were met with groans and boos.

"No other business treats its major outlet so badly," New York exhibitor Martin Levine has said.

Major outlet? A running dispute between distributors and theater owners is over how important cinemas really are. MPPA figures show the majors earning only 34 percent of their total revenue from domestic theatrical grosses, while exhibitors' counter-figures claim that "less than 10 percent of the film companies' receipts come from other sources."

Imperceptibly, nontheatrical revenues increase. Theater owners know that and, through NATO, maintain a strong lobby against such "encroachments" as pay and cable television. But with sponsors paying $63,000 a minute for network prime time and producers getting upwards of $200,000 per Movie of the Week installment, electronics play an ever-increasing role. Universal's television film output is twice its theatrical film production and is actually keeping the huge studio tooled up and busy. The day MGM announced its withdrawal from distribution, it increased its emphasis on TV production by announcing twenty-eight pilot programs in development.

Nontheatrical films are in themselves a billion-dollar industry, and TV syndication is, again, a worldwide enterprise, with the American majors the main purveyors of entertainment series to the world's nearly 18,000 television stations.[4]

"Looking ten to twenty years into the future, I don't think the major studios are going to fold, although one or two of the conglomerates might decide to phase out their unprofitable filmmaking subsidiaries," is the considered opinion of Roger Corman. "The majors are handling financing and distribution rather well overall, but there is still a lot of waste."

The waste Corman and other longtime independents condemn is more the result of inefficiency than dishonesty. "If you have a bomb you still have to pay your distribution people, and when you have a hit you still need them," adds Corman.

The idea of a clearing-house concept of a flexible central financial

4. There are 248,000 commercially operated cinemas in the world, accommodating 27 filmgoers for every thousand of the world's population, according to UNESCO, but there are 17,630 television stations and 261 million TV sets. That is 70 sets per thousand people.

organization has been around for a decade—as has the idea of consolidating production under one gigantic studio roof. A super–distributing organization, however, is an idea whose time has not yet come. "Cutting distribution costs is as much of a factor as trimming production costs," said *Variety* publisher Thomas M. Pryor in commenting on MGM's decision to pull out. "There is no question that millions of dollars yearly go into the maintenance of duplication of physical handling of pictures into theaters and in making collections and that, mathematically at least, it should be cheaper through a centralized agency." [5]

A radical solution might be to abandon fixed boxoffice prices. "The motion-picture industry runs the only retail business that openly and without compunction charges its customers the same high prices for inferior product as it does for quality product," wrote veteran trade-paper editor Don Carle Gillette in 1974, insisting that this inconsistency could be the most important hidden factor responsible for the perpetual ups and downs and the decline of movie attendance. [6]

Another solution might be to seek U.S. government permission for a return to the good old days when the majors were allowed to own their own theaters. The Truman Administration broke up the majors' control of both production and exhibition in 1948. After years of antitrust litigation, the justice department won a series of consent decrees that forced the majors to sell their chains of movie houses. In terms of strict idealism, the action was perfectly sound in 1948, but, as Charles Higham has said, "in practical terms, the victory of the Department of Justice and the independents over wicked Hollywood had incalculably disastrous effects on the film industry and the very character of film entertainment itself. For confidence in a product, the feeling that it could flow out along guaranteed lines of distribution, was what gave many Hollywood films before 1948 their superb attack and vigor. Also, the block booking custom, evil though it may have been, ensured that many obscure, personal and fascinating movies could be made and released, featherbedded by the system and underwritten by more conventional ventures." [7]

The mid-1970s are not the high 40s, and there have been half-

5. *Variety*, Sept. 18, 1973.
6. *Journal of the Producers' Guild of America*, June 1974.
7. Charles Higham, *Hollywood at Sunset*. New York: Saturday Review Press, 1972.

hearted attempts at making Washington change its policy. In 1971 Columbia and Warner's became the joint owners of The Burbank Studio (formerly the WB plant), and to further trim overheads and share costs began distributing features abroad under one banner. In 1973, when Columbia announced a three-year fiscal loss of $82 million, the company was seeking a domestic arrangement with another distributor. Cinerama, also a firm in less than happy financial straits, was a likely candidate, and it was felt that because both companies had had losing years, the justice department might give favorable consideration to such an arrangement. A year later, the federal government eased the consent decrees somewhat by allowing Loews, Inc., ABC Theaters, Mann Theaters, and Cinerama Releasing's subsidiary, RKO–Stanley Warner Theaters, to build new moviehouses without obtaining government permission (the acquisition of existing theaters would still require justice-department consent). The removal of this restraint was expected to result in a massive building boom, although many theatermen cautioned that the problem was not too few screens but too few films. "Where the pictures are going to come from to feed all these screens is unknown at this time, as I see it," said Pacific Theaters president Robert Selig the day after the justice-department action.

Still another new-old idea making exhibitors sit up and take notice is the "pushcart," or outright sales, practice revived by George C. Scott for his independently financed *The Savage Is Loose*. Completely bypassing the majors, producer-director-star Scott and his backers sold the picture outright to a 170-theater chain in Chicago for a flat fee and no percentages and followed up with other territorial deals. Features had been handled in this manner until 1915, when the majors began to buy into strategic locations and, when competition stiffened further, to build their own theaters.

Scott is not the only Hollywoodite making the rounds personally to peddle his film to theater owners. Tom Laughlin and Dolores Taylor, the husband-wife team who are stars and producers of the hugely successful *Billy Jack* and its sequel, were the first to make direct deals with theater and circuit owners. For his "tough sell" *A Woman Under the Influence*, John Cassavetes opened the picture by renting Manhattan's Columbia I and II theaters himself. Francis Ford Coppola, whose directing of *The Godfather* made him a millionaire, has acquired controlling interest in Cinema 5, a distribution company which also owns fifteen choice New York theaters.

"I hope to see distribution in the hands of men who really like film," says Coppola, "not people who treat filmmakers as children they have to keep around."

Meanwhile, the justice department's overseers of the film business attend NATO functions and rule on such issues as whether film "tracks"—preset groups of houses playing pictures according to locally defined rules—constitute block booking or whether a distributor preselecting a theater in a given area without open bidding means a violation of antitrust laws. The consent decrees have never had any effect on theater chains outside the United States. Paramount owns more than 300 houses in Canada and key cinemas in France, for example, while Fox owns chains in Australia, Britain, and France.

"If I were on Broadway," Houston's Alley Theater director Nina Vance has said, "I'd have to think that my horse was going to come first every time. But to do that six or eight times a year is impossible."

Impossible or not, that is almost par for Disney, UA, Warner's, Fox, Paramount, Columbia, and Universal, and in 1974 there were indications that the boom-or-bust attendance of recent years was leveling off and that more films were sharing the boxoffice. Sober forecasts see the movies more than holding their own over the coming years.

10

Bogdanovich and Coppola

THE HOTTEST YOUNG FILMMAKERS in America are a pair of clever Hollywoodites who have little in common except that they are both deadly serious about films and filming and, way back, got their first chances from the same low-budget entrepreneur. They are two articulate pop artists of a kind the industry wouldn't have tolerated a few years ago. After only a handful of films each, they are a pair of right-on millionaires who have achieved poise, presence, clout, and personality.

Peter Bogdanovich is the only American film critic to have made the leap to Big Time directing, and Francis Ford Coppola is the first graduate of *any* university cinema department to make it. Bogdanovich is a believer in sheen and professionalism, and Coppola is an Oscarized *auteur* dedicated to high-risk commercial movies. Both are much too successful to be your average American filmmaker under thirty-five, but their timing, trials, and triumphs make them textbook cases of young directors' ascents in the 1970s.

When Coppola was twenty-three and fresh out of the University of California at Los Angeles (UCLA), he conned Roger Corman into letting him spend $20,000 left from a horror classic to make something called *Dementia*. Ten years later, he was a rumpled teddy bear behind shaggy beard and smoked spectacles, living with his wife, Eleanor, and their children—two boys and a baby girl—in an ornate nineteenth-century spice king's San Francisco castle in a creative collision of Juan Miro paintings, art gallery chic, and scarlet kids' tricycles. When Bogdanovich was twenty-six he managed to convince Corman to let him direct Boris Karloff in a piece of Hitchockery called *Targets*. Eight years later, he had succeeded in accomplishing his wildest dreams, voluptuously talking million-dollar budgets and running movies in the private screening room of an immaculate Bel Air mansion containing, among other prizes, Cybill Shepherd, the girl with wide sapphire eyes he discovered and made a movie queen.

By going against the grain of contemporary tastes and tics and realizing that the most audacious innovation might be to be old-fashioned, Bogdanovich hit the bull's-eye with his second picture and made two more superhits in a row. When he proposed *The Last Picture Show* to BBS Productions, the short-lived Columbia farm club for hip young men of independent means was drowning in money and fame for having produced *Easy Rider*. But Bogdanovich told BBS chief Bert Schneider that what he had in mind was not a counterculture manifesto about a spaced-out pop saint, but a black-and-white movie about the 1950s. About what? About the end of an era, about outgrowing painful adolescence, in short about life-styles and attitudes practically vanished from the national con-science. When he was being lionized at the New York film festival a year later for *The Last Picture Show*, Bogdanovich didn't howl with the hirsute firebrands and proclaim himself instant genius. Instead, he paid tribute to the old masters—Hitchcock, Hawks, and Ford—and said all the great movies already had been made.

The son of a Serbian painter who fled Yugoslavia in 1939 with his pregnant Austrian-Jewish wife, Bogdanovich is a self-confessed child of the cinema, a true movie freak who can boast of having seen seven thousand movies (it takes almost three films a day to see a thousand a year). Since high school, Bogdanovich has written film reviews, and between the ages of twelve and thirty he kept an index-card file on every movie he had seen. His literary swash-buckling includes articles on Jerry Lewis, Humphrey Bogart, James Stewart, Cary Grant, and scores of other stars; interview paperbacks on John Ford and Fritz Lang (the latter volume against Lang's wishes); and monographs on Alfred Hitchcock and Howard Hawks. For a while he wrote a Hollywood column for *Esquire*, and his byline has appeared in every sort of publication, from *Cahiers du Cinéma* to *The Saturday Evening Post*. He has programmed retrospec-tives and festivals for the New York Museum of Modern Art and the American Film Institute. He remembers in detail who knocked him on the way up and is quick to talk about his own gifts and equally quick to show contempt for other young filmmakers. "I have a perverse antagonism for the 'new' movie," he told *Newsweek* in 1971. "My instinct is to reject all those modern techniques. In too many movies the camera is the star." [1] Two years later he said it better: "The point is that my emotional preference is older movies. I don't want to make a movie like the ones that I don't like today, that I don't respond to emotionally. A lot of modern stories are about alienation, so they tend to alienate the audience. Purposely, but I don't like that. I really want to be swept along."

Bogdanovich identifies with the story and the star. "Movie stars form a kind of twentieth-century mythology—they are the Greek gods to us," he told Digby Diehl after he had made *What's Up, Doc?* "The fact remains that every so often in pictures there comes a person, male or female, who has some certain something which is totally undefinable, which is fascinating. And he will become a star because he's interesting to look at." [2]

Bogdanovich, who was born in Kingston, New York, and grew up in Manhattan, never dreamed of being a critic or director. He wanted to be an actor. In school, he acted in the drama club and produced a movie and theater column in the school newspaper. At nineteen, he wrote an impassioned letter to Clifford Odets asking for permission to direct his play, *The Big Knife*. Odets gave him the go-ahead, and Bogdanovich was to remember Carroll O'Connor, one of his stars: "We had an argument. He had a lot of dialogue and was always smoking a cigar during rehearsals. I told him not to smoke so much. He didn't."

When Universal was about to release *The Birds*, Bogdanovich persuaded the studio to share the cost of a Hitchcock retrospective. He did much the same for Howard Hawks, "because I wanted to see all his films." In 1964 Bogdanovich and his wife, Polly, moved west to conquer Hollywood. Roger Corman, who over the years has given a lot of cinema students their first chance, put Peter to work on *The Wild Angels*. The film was directed by Corman himself, a sordid story of motorcycle-gang violence with a semidocumentary style and an innovative use of rock music on the sound track. The year was 1966.

1. *Newsweek*, Oct. 18, 1971.
2. *Los Angeles Times*, Apr. 2, 1972.

Next, the "king of the B's" asked Bogdanovich to shoot additional scenes for *Storm Clouds of Venus*, a Russian science-fiction film
to which he owned the American rights. AIP would release it, he
told Bogdanovich, for the special effects if there was some sex in it.
"So Mamie van Doren and seven pubescent ladies were hired,"
Peter remembered. "They were all blonde because I thought everybody should be blonde on Venus. I dressed them up in rubber
suits—bottoms only, and put shells over their breasts. I had them
traipsing around Carrillo Beach for a while shooting inserts that
might relate to Venus."

Bogdanovich put the hodgepodge together, but when AIP executives couldn't figure out what was going on, he put in thought-
voices to explain the monsters, the astronauts, and the Venusian
ladies. When it still didn't make sense, he had the best-looking
earthling narrate the picture. The end result was *Voyage to the Planet
of the Prehistoric Women*, a picture that was never released theatri-
cally but can still be seen on late-night TV.

Corman offered Bogdanovich a chance to direct—on two conditions: that he use Boris Karloff, who owed Corman two days of
shooting, and that the film include outtakes from the Karloff-starrer
The Terror. The result was *Targets*, the story of a clean-cut Califor-
nian youth going off his rocker (Tom O'Kelly) and killing wife,
mother, and a grocer's delivery boy before packing his armory into
his car and from a sniper's vantage point overlooking a freeway
gunning down everything that moves. The fabricated horror of
Karloff movies and the sniper's real-life horror come together in the
end when the mad youth sets himself up in a drive-in and is literally *in* the Karloff movie. He sits behind the drive-in screen, pokes
a hole in it, and fires at the audience.

Although *Targets* was critically well-received, it didn't lead directly to the next film. For a few years, Bogdanovich was back
writing film library brochures and, with an American Film Institute (AFI) grant, conducting in-depth tape interviews with John
Ford. These sessions led to *Directed by John Ford*, Bogdanovich's
only documentary, in which the master deflects questions about his
oeuvre with "Yeah," "No" and "Cut!" The ninety-minute documentary, which also had John Wayne, James Stewart, and Henry
Fonda discuss Ford with terror and awe, was financed with a
$29,000 grant from the California Arts Commission as part of its
belated backyard *kultur* discoveries.

What drew Bogdanovich to Larry McMurty's 1950 novel *The Last Picture Show* was the period and the idea of using old movies, TV clips, and vintage hit records to make a Texas version of Orson Welles's adaptation of Booth Tarkington's *The Magnificent Ambersons*, also a study in decline. "In a way, the television sets in *The Last Picture Show* herald the end of an era for me in the same way that the automobile signified the end of an era in *The Magnificent Ambersons*," he said—an utterance that was unfairly turned around to mean that Bogdanovich was out to copy the Welles classic.

Director and novelist (*Horseman, Pass By* is another McMurty book that, as *Hud*, achieved fame as a movie) scouted Texas, settled on the writer's hometown of Thalia, and fictionalized it to Anarene. Bogdanovich shot some footage of the town in color and found the hues made the town look pretty. He managed to convince BBS's Schneider to let him shoot in black-and-white. Robert Surtees was on camera, Polly designed the production. Filming was not pleasant. Peter and Polly became estranged and Bogdanovich's father died during the shooting.

The cast was made up of newcomers and established bit-part players—Timothy Bottoms and Jeff Bridges as the small-town All-American teen-age hero and his hard-luck buddy; Cybill Shepherd as the high school tease; Ben Johnson as father figure, picture show owner, and last link to the frontier past; Ellen Burstyn as a tough, middle-aged beauty; and Cloris Leachman as perhaps the screen's least glamorous adultress.

Peter's first meeting with Cybill was not something out of a Bogdanovich movie. "Cybill sat on the floor and seemed totally bored," he recalled a few years later. "I asked her what she did, and she said that she went to college and that she liked to read. I asked her who her favorite author was and she said Dostoevsky. Then, when I asked which of his books she liked best, she said, after a long pause, 'Well, I can't think of anything right now.' However, she was toying with the flowers in a vase, and there was something so casually destructive about it, it seemed to imply the kind of woman who doesn't mean to be cruel to men, but who is."

Bogdanovich's feat in *The Last Picture Show* was tone, wistful straightforwardness, and brilliant understatement. He never mingled his characters' nostalgia with his own, never allowed his regret for vanished worlds and wasted opportunities to intrude. He cut out what didn't advance the plot.

In a long and generous review, Andrew Sarris said the film's popularity was probably due to its upbeat message. "There is something in it for which a great many people have been waiting for a long time, possibly the exact opposite of what Dennis Hopper thought people were waiting for when he was working on *The Last Movie*," Sarris wrote. "As Hopper's movie is the ultimate expression of self-hatred, Bogdanovich's picture is the ultimate expression of self-esteem. And I suspect people have had their fill of self-hatred. Both the Hopper and the Bogdanovich have the word 'last' in their titles, but only the Hopper is genuinely apocalyptic. If our civilization is indeed coming to an end, the fact that there will be no more new movies is the least of our problem. If our civilization is not coming to an end, movies that say it is sound fatuously self-indulgent and pointlessly pessimistic. . . . What shines through *The Last Picture Show* is not so much the heroism of the characters as their capacity for survival. . . . It is to Bogdanovich's credit and profit that he has managed at one and the same time to turn out an extraordinarily good movie and a refreshing affirmation of the life force of our civilization." [3]

After *The Last Picture Show*, Bogdanovich could write his own ticket—and did. Before *The Last Picture Show* was in release, Sue Mengers got him the directing job on what ultimately became *What's Up, Doc?*, for which Barbra Streisand and Ryan O'Neal had already been packaged. Streisand owned a piece of the expensive ($4.6 million) flick, and with grosses of more than $30 million, her cut of the profits was the best she had ever managed.

What's Up, Doc? (which is not what the company first set out to film) looked suspiciously like Hawks's 1938 Katharine Hepburn–Cary Grant screwball comedy *Bringing Up Baby*, in which Cary Grant played a paleontologist and Katharine Hepburn a millionaire lawyer's daughter. Not surprisingly. "I sent the script to Howard Hawks, who said, 'Pretty good, but you haven't got anything as good as the dinosaur,' " Bogdanovich said during filming. "I said, 'I know, Howard, but I couldn't steal *that!*' "

Before they started filming, Bogdanovich sent O'Neal to talk to Grant, while he pumped Hawks. "I think Cary told him not to comment on the comedy, just play it straight, which is just about the same thing Hawks told me. His only comment was, 'Don't let them be cute.' "

3. *Village Voice*, Oct. 14, 1971.

Again with O'Neal as his leading man—and O'Neal's daughter Tatum as a roguish nine-year-old—Bogdanovich next made another money winner. Again filmed in black-and-white, *Paper Moon* was another rear-mirror glance, this time a 1930s Shirley Temple movie about a con artist hustling Bibles to widows and a flinty-eyed nine-year-old orphan stealing the show. Polly was the production designer again, and together with Laszlo Kovacs' cinematography of Kansas flatlands, her careful, decorous sets of Depression landscapes lent credence to the tawdry story.

Paper Moon was produced by The Directors' Company, a corporate entity created in association with Paramount by Bogdanovich, Coppola, and William Friedkin (then of *The French Connection* fame). To fight studio autocracy, directors had tried to band together as early as 1931, when Cecil B. DeMille, Frank Borzage, Lewis Milestone, and King Vidor tried and failed to form an independent group called The Directors' Guild. After World War II, the most famous attempt was Liberty Films, which united Frank Capra, George Stevens, and William Wyler, and was swallowed up by Paramount after Capra's two first Liberty movies proved commercial flops.

The aims of the Paramount-Bogdanovich-Coppola-Friedkin alliance were to afford creative autonomy once a project was approved, to encourage "cross-pollination," and to enable the three directors to share financially in each other's successes (what about each other's disasters?). Three Paramount executives—Frank Yablans, Robert Evans, and the "resident intellectual," Peter Bart—sat on the board along with the three filmmakers. To be approved, a project required a majority vote, and in early meetings neither directors nor company men voted together as a bloc. "In terms of deal, both Paramount and the three filmmakers have made certain short-term financial sacrifices in an effort to make the company a viable economic entity," Bart said when the firm was launched in 1972.

Bogdanovich's second Directors' Company film was *Daisy Miller*, an adaptation of Henry James's 1878 novella—the story of a rich American girl colliding with European high society. Probably James's most popular single work in his lifetime, *Daisy Miller* was shot in Switzerland and Italy, with Cybill Shepherd in the title role, Cloris Leachman playing her mother, Barry Brown as a captivated young man, and Larry McMurty's son, James, as Daisy's bratty kid brother.

"It's a period very much removed from anything I've known,"

Bogdanovich said in setside interviews. "It's a very delicate type of social tragedy about manners and morals. It's about innocence—not, unfortunately, a very vital subject these days. I don't know if people will give a damn. I do. But that's what it's about, and missed opportunities, too. The movie's rather more ambiguous than the book, I'm afraid."

"It's the first time I've made a picture that's beautiful to look at, that *had* to be beautiful to look at. Part of the sadness of the story is it's so beautiful."

After *Daisy Miller*, Bogdanovich moved to Fox to do the expensive musical fantasy *At Long Last Love*—or *ALLL*, as he calls it—a 1931 Broadway musical fantasy awash with Cole Porter tunes and starring Burt Reynolds and Cybill Shepherd. It was to be followed by a ganster flick, *Bugsy*, the story of mobster Bugsy Siegel, who was mysteriously murdered in the late 1940s. Bankrolled by Universal, *Bugsy* (once a Tony Curtis project) was to be filmed from a screenplay by *Great White Hope* playwright Howard Sackler.

"I make an active effort," says Bogdanovich, "to preserve my innocence about story as well as about filmmaking as such. With each succeeding picture, I try more consciously to rely on my instinct and to listen to my instinct as much as possible."

Between films, Peter and Cybill live self-indulgently at the former Kay Gable estate he acquired with *Paper Moon*, showing movies almost nightly in the special screening room, buying furniture impulsively, and enlarging the Beverly Hills house to include rooms for his two visiting daughters, aged seven and four. "We have absolutely no thoughts of being married," Cybill tells columnists, to which he nods, "Does she look like Mrs. Bogdanovich?" They are both sought for starring roles in pictures he wouldn't necessarily direct (he was last *before* the cameras costarring with John Huston in Orson Welles's three-years-in-the-making *The Other Side of the Wind*).

"I'm not playing up that part of my career, but what's a fella to do?" he says. He isn't casting himself in his own pictures, saying he hasn't got the nerve to do that. "I did it in *Targets* and that was my only failure."

Bogdanovich, who helped finance *The Other Side of the Wind*, now regrets having so freely acknowledged the influences of Welles, Hawks, and Ford, and says he now realizes a director is someone who presides over accidents. "I don't put a very high premium on originality for its own sake because I don't think there's anything original anymore," he said during the filming of *Daisy Miller*. "Part of the great thing about civilization is it's a growing and evolving thing. Nothing irritates me more than saying history and tradition don't matter.

"There's a wonderful line in *A Streetcar Named Desire* where Blanche says we haven't come far in this mysterious journey we're making from the caves, but let's not hang back with the brutes. That's totally misquoted, I'm afraid."

On Bogdanovich's busy schedule is also *Palo Duro*, a western written with McMurty, and an untitled Hollywood epic beginning in 1911 and going into the 1940s. "The birth of the movies is a kind of background for a story about a director, a kind of composite figure of four or five directors I've known."

The western would star James Stewart, John Wayne, and Henry Fonda. "Just to be able to say John Wayne, Jimmy Stewart, and Henry Fonda are in *my* movie. What a fantasy that is to live out!"

While Bogdanovich was finishing *Daisy Miller*, Coppola was running over budget shooting the sequel to his celebrated *Godfather*. Variously called *The Godfather II* and *The Godfather, Part II* during production, the expensive follow-up told the adventures of the next generation of the Corleone dynasty.

"All cinema should be marginal," Coppola has said, but he has never really labored in any 16-mm. twilight himself. He sold his first script when he was nineteen, directed his first feature when he was twenty-three, wrote *Patton* at twenty-six, and was a hip movie mogul at thirty. By the time he was thirty-three, he had his first crashing failure *behind* him.

"I was at UCLA film school from about 1960 to 1962 and I barely had two friends in that time," the son of the solo flutist in Arturo Toscanini's NBC Symphony Orchestra told Stephen Farber after *The Godfather*. "My fantasy was you're working on the films and drinking wine at night, and there are beautiful girls who are working on the films and you're all in it together. It wasn't like that. It was very lonely. However, there was the chance to learn about some of the technology. There were a couple of good courses. One was my directing teacher, Dorothy Arzner, and she was always very sweet to me and encouraging. She was one of the better influences." [4]

4. *Sight and Sound*, autumn 1972.

After graduating, the Detroit-born Coppola became another hopeful getting a first job at the Corman factory. (Corman in 1969: "I think it's worthwhile to help the young person of some talent to get started in films; it's enjoyable and stimulating and I generally have made money at it, although recently the margin of profit has dropped.") When Coppola had proved himself, Corman took him with him to London, where the Edgar Allan Poe chillers and other quickies were sometimes made. Coppola became dialogue director and assistant-to-everybody on three Corman pictures: *Tower of London*, *Premature Burial*, and a car-racing thriller shot in five days, *Young Racers*.

"Somehow there was $20,000 left over when we were through," Francis said in 1966. "I asked Roger to let me make a picture for that $20,000 and he agreed on the condition that I make it in Ireland and in less than ten days. He gave me a secretary who was supposed to cosign all checks and off we went. In Dublin, I immediately had the girl sign a check for the whole amount, which I put in an account under my own name. Corman flew to America and I wrote the screenplay directly on mimeo stencils." [5]

"Just before the shooting started, Raymond Stross, the English producer, got interested in my film and I sold him the British rights for $20,000. Now I had $40,000. When Corman heard about this, he wanted to withdraw the initial production money, but I had put it in another account, remember. *Dementia*—yes, it was an appropriate title—was shot in seven days with Patrick McGee, Bill Campbell, and seven Irish players. Afterward, I was supposed to have made a picture in Yugoslavia, but I got married and came home."

For the next years, Coppola was a house writer of sorts for Seven Arts, which later merged with Warner Brothers. He turned out a dozen scripts, and one of his eye-openers was the Franco-American disaster *Is Paris Burning?* Francis spent months in Paris as the junior writer of an improbable quartet of scenarists. The others were Gore Vidal and two top French scripters, Jean Aurenche and Pierre Bost. In the face of producer Paul Graetz, director René Clément backed down too often and the whole production backed down in the face of a government scared to okay a film that might displease Charles de Gaulle. "I got into lots of arguments and was

5. *Los Angeles Times*, Jan. 2, 1966.

always fired," Coppola remembered. "There was really nothing to write about. You weren't even allowed to say the word 'Communist' in the script.

"For some stupid reason, Clément's contract didn't give him a say over the script, and for some equally stupid reason Graetz wanted to keep it that way. So, to circumscribe this, Clément's ideas were presented as mine at story conferences, and of course I didn't mind, since Clément's ideas invariably were the best."

To keep his sanity, Coppola wrote *You're A Big Boy Now*, a comedy in the vein of Richard Lester's Beatle froth, *A Hard Day's Night*, and when he got back from Paris he began a campaign to convince Seven Arts to let him direct it. Before getting behind the viewfinder, however, there was still another writing assignment (now that he was a World War II history expert). At Fox, producer Frank McCarthy had struggled through endless writers and drafts to get the story of George S. Patton off the ground. These efforts had been by men of McCarthy's own generation, writers who had known the war and Patton's awesome stature in American hierology. McCarthy's stroke of genius was to hire Coppola, who had been five when Patton died and who took the general for what he was—a magnificent anachronism. Only a twenty-five-year-old of Coppola's innocent irreverence could have mashed the heap of Patton wartime speeches and flinty scatology into the opening scene of the bemedaled and bepistoled general in front of a gigantic American flag exhorting his troops to be invincible savages.

By the time Franklin Schaffner began filming in 1969, Edmund North had done another polishing job on the script, but the *Patton* that became the freak hit during the darkest days of the Vietnam war was basically the samurai version Coppola had written.

Although Coppola would later return to the typewriter (after *The Godfather* he adapted F. Scott Fitzgerald's *The Great Gatsby* for Paramount), he came away from screenwriting with a rather low opinion of producers' and studios' idiosyncrasies. "Producers are stupid and insecure," he said in 1966. "They hire five different writers to do a screenplay and end up with five first drafts instead of one fifth draft."

Meanwhile, he began his next project, directing *You're A Big Boy Now*—a lesser anachronism, as it turned out, a piece of derivative moviemaking running the gamut of New Wave effects that might have been fresh when Coppola first tried to get Seven Arts behind it. As it was, it was a New York version of Lester's *The Knack*, the story of how one gets rid of one's virginity when one is the nineteen-year-old son of caricature parents. "I didn't enjoy doing the film," Coppola said five years later. "I think that was my fault. I was scared. My other experiences of directing have been very pleasurable. This time I was in New York, and it was a real union crew, and I had a limited schedule."

Peter Kastner played the gap-toothed Bernard Chanticleer, who, when he was not rollerskating through the New York Public Library, where he worked for Father (Rip Torn), was at home with Mother (Geraldine Page). The rest of the cast included Julie Harris as Bernard's landlady when he moved away from his anxious and possessive mother and Elizabeth Hartman as the very off-Broadway actress who finally deflowered our hero. *You're A Big Boy Now* was totally eclipsed by Mike Nichols' *The Graduate*. It became Coppola's master's thesis at UCLA.

In 1968, Coppola was picked to direct *Finian's Rainbow* and *Mame*. Warner Brothers executives felt the only way these properties could be brought to the screen would be by a very young director. When Coppola got *Finian's Rainbow*, he took one look and decided there was no way to modernize it without destroying it. "I tried to shoot it for what it was—an old, outdated, but totally lovable musical. The score was great, but this mixture of a leprechaun and God and a tame civil rights message—it was just the wrong time to make a movie like that."

Warner executives, however, were happy enough with Petula Clark's singing and Fred Astaire's tap dancing, and the touch of asperity that Coppola had managed, to give it a 70-mm. roadshow launch. "The studio next wanted me to do *Mame*, offered me almost $400,000 back then, when I was twenty-six or twenty-seven years old. And I had this brilliant idea: I'm going to force the case, I'm going to do *The Rain People* instead. By just starting to do it, I'll prevent myself from succumbing to all these offers."

The Rain People, which Coppola had originally written in creative-writing class, was a "road picture," an excursion into American alienation and anomie that cost $700,000 and was a financial disaster. Coppola jumped into it without a finished script. He had been captivated by Shirley Knight. "I didn't know her, but I thought she was very good. She seemed like an American actress who had some substance. The idea of writing a film for an actress and making it

Contemporary urban hero: George Segal in *The Black Bird, Or The Maltese Falcon Flies Again*.

Bond forever: Roger Moore, surrounded by Maud Adams and Britt Ekland in *The Man With the Golden Gun*.

"I'm kind of proletarian, interested in people with limited choices": David S. Ward receiving the 1973 writing Oscar for *The Sting*.

Above: A scene from the hot ($300,000) original script *Yakuza*, with Robert Mitchum.

Below: Feminine rewriting—Kris Kristofferson, Ellen Burstyn, and Martin Scorsese on *Alice Doesn't Live Here Anymore*.

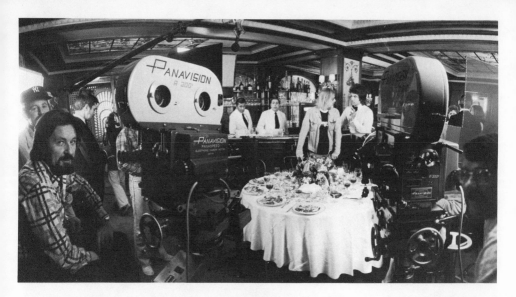

"Who has ever heard of a violin operator?" Laszlo Kovacs (left) behind Panavision camera waiting for director Hal Ashby and Warren Beatty (center) to roll a take on *Shampoo*.

Praise and blame fall increasingly on his shoulders: George Roy Hill filming *Slaughterhouse Five*.

Moviemaking is also a nine-to-five livelihood for tens of thousands. Stuntmen working on Norman Jewison's *Rollerball*.

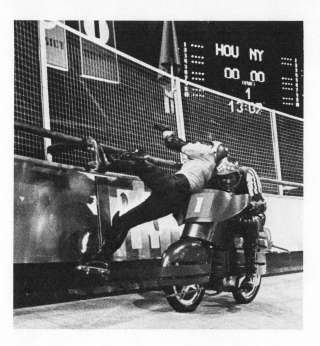

Independent "pickup": Brian de Palma's rock fantasy *Phantom of The Paradise*, starring Paul Williams, became a Twentieth Century–Fox release.

Peter Bogdanovich directing Burt Reynolds and Cybill Shepherd in *At Long Last Love*.

"It's ironic, but the new interest in films has a tendency to eliminate, not to encourage, first efforts." Mr. and Mrs. Irwin Winkler (left) and Mr. and Mrs. Robert Chartoff on the set of the Chartoff-Winkler production *Fat Chance*.

Up from porn: fully clothed Linda Lovelace in *Linda Lovelace for President*.

"To be a director is like running in front of a locomotive—if you stop, if you trip, if you make a mistake, you get killed." Above: Francis Ford Coppola with Gene Hackman on *The Conversation*.

Below: Clarice Taylor and Virginia Capers in *Five on the Black Hand Side*—an untried genre, black ethnic humor.

together, like Antonioni with Monica Vitti, really appealed to me."

The Rain People, which has remained Coppola's own favorite, has wayward Shirley Knight meet James Caan as a punchy jock and Robert Duvall as a lecherous state trooper. The film was most notable for Coppola's production technique. Using a small crew, he loaded everybody on station wagons and Cinemobile trucks and shot the movie through eighteen states, picking his locations as he went. "There are those of us who still talk about the cookouts in the back of the sound truck," Caan recalled when they were making *Godfather II*. Francis even had a twenty-two-year-old University of Southern California cinema graduate, George Lucas, shooting a film of the filming. But he didn't get along with his leading lady. "Whenever an actor starts to distrust the director, he begins to do two things—he's acting and he's also watching out for himself. I don't think Shirley Knight trusted me. I don't think she felt that if she did what I asked her to do it would be a good movie."

Next, Francis declared Hollywood a wasteland and moved to San Francisco to set himself up in his own studio. The trade press, Sunday supplements, slicks, and underground and buff magazines soon reported enthusiastically on the freebooters' haven on Folsom Street, describing the three crayon-colored floors of the converted warehouse, jam-packed with the latest in sophisticated equipment, projection and screening rooms, editing rooms, and an art department. (Coppola: "Film students walk in and get weak in the knees.") Everybody admired Francis for his formidable ripoff of Hollywood. Warner Brothers more or less financed the whole thing.

It all looked too good to believe, terribly chic and terribly sincere, with leggy secretaries in crocheted miniskirts, $50,000 Kem and Steenbeck editing tables, Creative Playthings paraphernalia, bubbly chairs, and blowups of D. W. Griffith on the walls. After toying with Trans-America Sprocket Works, Coppola named his outfit American Zoetrope (Greek for life and movement and the name of the slotted revolving drum that preceded the invention of the kinematoscope). AZ drew "crowds" of newcomers to the Bay Area. Stanley Kubrick and Francis exchanged weekly letters on post–*2001, A Space Odyssey* techniques, John Schlesinger expressed interest, Mike Nichols asked how he could invest in American Zoetrope, Haskell Wexler planned to base his new company on Folsom Street, John Korty leased a set of offices, and even Orson Welles was going to do a film with Zoetrope. Only one film was actually made—Lucas' *THX 1138*, the closest thing to an American *film maudit*, an instant flop that Warner Brothers hated and that went on to become a kind of cult film.

One by one, nine projects "firmed up" with Warner's were dropped. To keep afloat, Zoetrope grabbed onto TV commercials (Rice-A-Roni, Saffola) and set up an advertising division as well as Trimedia, an educational film service, but Coppola had to mothball the whole operation and, a little older and wiser and a lot poorer, return south to direct *The Godfather* for Paramount. "I had to take it. I was in trouble. I had sunk all my bread into Zoetrope and I owed a lot of money."

The Godfather, that preposterous all-time smash hit, changed everything again. As the Corleone saga edged toward inflationary blockbusterdom approaching a quarter of a billion dollars in worldwide grosses and Francis himself became a millionaire, he could reactivate Zoetrope as a rental facility and personally envisage a different future. Suddenly, financial pressures were off for good, and, at thirty-three, he could reorient his life and change priorities and motivations.

Coppola's attitudes toward *The Godfather* have remained both enthusiastic and defensive. It was quite an experience. Paramount began by saying no to a lot of things—to casting Brando and Al Pacino, to filming the epic in period, to location shooting in Sicily. Everyone hated Brando on the first day, and Paramount production chief Robert Evans made inquiries to see whether Elia Kazan was available to replace Coppola. Francis had told Paramount it would take eighty days to shoot and he was given a fifty-five-day schedule. As he fell one day behind every week, he was almost fired. After three weeks, however, he had a decisive meeting with Gulf & Western chief Charles Bluhdorn, who came to his support.

Coppola had been told in no uncertain terms that if he came in with a final cut longer than two and a half hours, they would pull the whole thing from under him. His director's cut was much shorter than the film actually released. "I have to give Bob Evans credit there," Coppola said. "As soon as he saw the film, he decided it would be a major hit. He staked his career on it, because he was the guy who fought for the length. The final cut is pretty close to everything I had shot, but there was some beautiful Sicilian footage removed, a scene in which James Caan tells his mother that his father is dead, which didn't work on the screen."

"I feel that a great deal of my background as an Italian-American with very strong memories about family rituals, the weddings, the funerals, went into the picture," Francis told Charles Higham in 1973. "I was deeply anxious to show that world as it is, not as it's often portrayed. But of course there's no doubt there's more of Mario Puzo in the picture than anybody else. The film, after all, is extremely faithful to the book.[6]

Although he admitted that Brando's Corleone might play a shade too snugly to popular Mafia mythology, Coppola didn't feel that *The Godfather* was too sympathetic to organized crime. "After all, at the end of the picture we see Michael (Pacino) telling a mortal lie to his wife. We see that after everything has happened he's no longer a man, he's a monster. The film doesn't soften that, or sentimentalize that. It shuts the door right in your face."

Before *Godfather II*, Coppola made *The Conversation*, a thriller about the nightmare threat of electronic eavesdropping. "I had been terrified by the whole Orwellian dimension of electronic spying and the invasion of privacy when I started writing *The Conversation* five years ago," he said when the nation held its breath over Watergate. "I realized a bugging expert was a special breed of man, not just a private eye playing with far-out gadgets."

Gene Hackman plays the San Francisco bugging expert, and Cindy Williams and Frederick Forrest the couple whose conversation he is paid $15,000 to record. Throughout the film, Hackman's tape of the couple's seemingly casual talk in a city square is heard over and over and assumes different meanings.

If Brando had not been too angry with Paramount for publicly criticizing his refusal to accept his *Godfather* Oscar, the sequel would have had the same offhanded time structure as *The Conversation*, with the basic story set in different periods. When Coppola became convinced that Brando could not be persuaded to come back, he and Puzo began extensive revisions of their joint screenplay, writing Don Corleone out and shifting action and emphasis to the next generation. The Brando character was to remain in one flashback to his Sicilian youth, with a young look-alike playing the

6. *Action*, May–June 1973.

part. Coppola started filming October 1, 1973, and after a few weeks was already over budget, shooting expensive party scenes at Lake Tahoe and in the Bahamas. Shooting ended $8 million later the following June.

"I'm dealless and free," he sighed toward the end of the *Godfather II* ordeal. "I have a contract with The Directors' Company, but I have eight years to work that off. Perhaps I won't do anything for the next five years, then make three pictures in three years.

"Beyond any movies I may have made, the most significant fact of my brief career is that I brought some young directors the opportunity. The best thing about today is that young filmmakers help each other, offer real assistance to each other."

Coppola's decision to buy into Cinema 5 and to become a member of the board of the distributing firm may turn out to be his most significant nondirectorial move. Rather than "revolutionary," he has called the decision a means of creating an alternative for filmmakers. Cinema 5, he said in the fall of 1974, will not become "another major" but "just a small, classy operation, which will see to it that a film is better exposed in its initial release."

"My motive has been to bypass the kinds of deals filmmakers have to make," he added, "deals in which a filmmaker has to totally surrender ownership, final cut, any say in how a film is released, what the advertising is like, in order to get the dollars up front to make his movie."

Though he wants to "lay low" in San Francisco for a couple of years, he does have a "pet project." He refuses to reveal what it is apart from the fact that it is based on a real event that occurred in the 1940s. "It's ripe to be remembered," he told *Variety*'s Richard Albarino during *Godfather II*, "and very controversial." [7]

If *Godfather II* earns another fortune, will he direct part III, perhaps taking the Corleone grandchildren into the Nixon era? "God, I hope not," he says fervently.

Bogdanovich and Coppola may never be more than reasonably talented directors, but they nevertheless represent one of the main ingredients of cinematic staying power—persuasiveness. Filmmaking is not for the fainthearted or the solitary. The movies demand gregarious, persuasive, if not overpowering personalities. They demand guile, bounce, and gab.

7. *Variety*, Mar. 27, 1974.

11

Ad-pubbing, Cannes, Oscars

To sell the public on a movie is an exercise in topology, that strange world of fascinating and improbable shapes at the far reaches of modern mathematics. Selling a picture is a matter of twisting and stretching surfaces that were not there in the first place or turning them into forms that seem impossible. Like the special world of pure mathematics, "ad-pubbing," or advertising-publicity, ranges from seeming child's play to abstractions that leave even experts puzzled.

The idea is to create what New York ad-pubbers call "word of mouth" and their more concise German confreres in Frankfurt call a film's "second reality." Bernardo Bertolucci's *Last Tango in Paris* was such an "event," a piece of social science fiction that had a second reality before it possessed a first existence. Before its American premiere in February 1973, extravagant praise and even extravagant damnation had kicked off a storm of controversy and provoked public debate that reduced intellectuals to hysteria. The picture was already an "event" in France, breaking boxoffice records in Paris, and before that it had been seized by Italian authorities for "persistent delight in arousing base, libidinous instincts." By the time of its strategic $5-a-head, reserved-seat opening in a small New York East Side theater—the ultimate ad-pub twist: making it difficult to see—Pauline Kael had called it a breakthrough comparable in its effect on film to the effect on music of Igor Stravinsky's historic first performance of *Sacre du Printemps* in 1913, and United

Artists had reprinted her *New Yorker* review in its entirety in its advertising. Both *Time* and *Newsweek* had given *Tango* their covers, *Playboy* had appeared with a display of stills showing Marlon Brando and twenty-year-old ripe-bodied Maria Schneider cavorting in the nude. UA's ad-pub topper Gabe Sumner had arranged exclusive pre-launch screenings (refusing Rex Reed admission to the press screening became itself the subject of a *Village Voice* column). Talk-show celebrities who had attended a screening couldn't wait to enliven their late-night blather with a titter or two about one of *Tango*'s sex scenes. The fact that they hadn't seen the film didn't stop columnist William F. Buckley, Jr., and ABC commentator Harry Reasoner from denouncing it as pornography disguised as art, a debate that was carried over the pages of such diverse magazines as *Paris-Match*, *Ms.*, *Der Spiegel*, and *Rolling Stone*. *Il Messagero*'s New York correspondent had informed all Italy about *Last Tango* during its unique "sneak" at the 1972 New York film festival and already forewarned it would have difficulties with Italian censors. In Rome, Alberto Moravia and Jesuit priest Domenico Grasso carried on a debate in the pages of *Corriere della Sera* (Moravia: "Sex is alive; everything else—the bourgeoisie, honor, order, family, marriage, even love—is dead." Father Grasso: "I deny that *everything* in human reality can be reduced to sex"). The Israeli censor's decision to let *Last Tango* pass uncut created a political sensation that nearly toppled the Golda Meir coalition government because of National Religious Party opposition to the film. Attendance to a Bertolucci press conference in London was such that UA sent out color-coded invitations (red for front-row scribes, blue for second bananas).

Before *Last Tango in Paris* opened in any territory, everyone knew what Marlon did and didn't do, about its heroine and her incessant private life, and about the director and his politics, his original and postdated intentions. The seconds the British censor snipped from the so-called butter scene were common knowledge to anyone in England, while in France the joke had *Tango* as the first Common Market production to help reduce the EEC butter surplus. Art Buchwald said the picture was about "the housing shortage in Paris and the lengths people will go to get an apartment," while a baker in Rome had himself arrested for selling entwined *Tango* breakfast rolls. In Milan twenty-four nightclubs went on a tango craze and played no other dance music, and Maurizio Bovarini came out with a comic strip takeoff "dedicated to those who have loved a lot, suffered more, and gone to the movies too often." In Germany a paperback retelling all these goings-on became a best seller.[1]

Although banned in many countries, notably Spain, Mexico, and most of South America, UA's earnings on the million-dollar production topped $20 million by the end of the first year in release.

"Event pictures" of the echo and magnitude of *Tango* are difficult to engineer. In 1974 Warner's had a money-jingling event picture in *The Exorcist*, but Paramount's remake of *The Great Gatsby* fell victim to its own publicity overkill and became "the movie to hate."

But ad-pubbing must also contend with more pedestrian screen-fare, films that need the push much more than movies rich in second-reality possibilities. The easiest way to create word of mouth is during shooting, and a film crew traditionally includes a publicist—more snazzily called *attaché de presse* on European productions. Although a declining art, unit publicity is by no means a hangover from the big studio days of ballyhoo and hokum. The need for publicity, from the inception of a movie to its release, is as great as ever, even if old-style mimeographed location stories marked "exclusive to your city" accompanied by a couple of 8-by-10 glossies no longer get automatic space in Sunday editions across the country.

"More junk mail isn't needed. Right now I toss most of it out without opening it because I know the routine of studio and producer mailings," *Milwaukee Journal* entertainment editor Alex Thien wrote in answer to a 1972 Publicists' Guild survey of print media editors. "What we need is pictures and information ten days preceding the Sunday after which the film will open," wrote *The San Francisco Chronicle's* Paine Knickerbocker. "This is something that many distributors ignore, missing a fat chance for available space and ink." United Features Syndicate writer Joseph Bell put it even more bluntly. "It is, of course, impossible to measure the effect of cumulative publicity, but the attitude that production stories are a waste of time and money and unit men are therefore unnecessary is, in my view as a reporter, tremendously shortsighted. The stories I can sell are production stories. I'm not in the business to serve as an ancillary publicity agent for film producers when it serves *their* fancy, e.g., *after* a film is in release. After all, filmmakers are ostensibly in business to sell films, not to inflate per-

1. Florian Hopf, *Alles über "Der Letzte Tango in Paris."* Munich: Wilhelm Heyne Verlag, 1973.

sonal egos by using part-time publicity men in a frantic prerelease effort to get mention of a producer in the trade press or in New York and Los Angeles newspapers. There are a hell of a lot of people between the coasts who buy tickets to movies." When asked for examples of films that were helped or hindered by publicity or lack thereof, Carole Kass of *The Richmond Times-Dispatch* offered, "With practically no material, except an occasional press book, I have not been able to 'help' any film lately."

One of the fixations of the film industry is that executives, directors, stars, and laborers all feel they are experts in two fields—their own and publicity. During the 1970 Hollywood recession, publicity departments were the first to be decimated. Ironically, most laid-off publicists eventually found work in television, a medium which appeals to what is fundamentally a "free" market and doesn't have to attract paying customers.

Ideally, a unit publicist is signed on along with the rest of the crew and stays on through production and sometimes even postproduction right up to the release. During the long months of filming on a bare-faced mountainside in Spain or deep in Bryce Canyon, Utah, the unit publicist is in a sense the only link with civilization. Depending on the publicity budget, he "junkets"—invites primadonna byliners, at company expense, to visit the location for interviews with stars and directors; he accumulates feature stories of shooting highlights that eventually become the bedrock of advertising and the "press book," that collection of screen facts, synopsis, and three-, two-, and one-column-inch ads which follows the movie to its last hinterland exhibitor. He directs the still photographer, tries to attract special-assignment photographers, and has a hand in making the free-lance or paid-for documentary on the shooting which often winds up as "clips" on TV public affairs and talk shows. He tells the studio home office when and when not to fly out news people (in case of open hostility on the set one week, visiting firemen are kept away). He "plants" trade press items on castings and runs a celebrity service on comings-and-goings. He writes fact sheets and captions photos, and in case of "negative vibes" (drunken driving arrests of the leading man or jealous scenes by the leading lady's husband) tries to keep the story out of the news.

Rona Barrett and Joyce Haber ply what's left of the gossip columnist's trade. Back when every girl wanted to be a movie star and knew the most likely route passed behind Schwab's soda fountain on Sunset Boulevard, she had an awesome need for gossip about filmdom's elite, their comings and goings, their love affairs and Terrible Secrets. In their prime Louella Parsons and Hedda Hopper possessed millions of breathlessly loyal readers, on whose behalf they arbitrarily controlled the fortunes of just about everybody involved in the industry. Louella retired in 1965, Hedda died the next year, and the vacuum has been filled, in a fashion, by Rona Barrett, Metromedia Television's gossip-in-residence, and *Los Angeles Times* syndicated columnist Joyce Haber. Most of the time they don't bother with the old-fashioned Parsons-Hopper pieties and voyeuristic common-scold admonitions. The new gossips smile and wink and swing with the crowd. They still use blind items ("A well-known actor . . ."), as does *Hollywood Reporter* columnist Hank Grant, whose showbiz chatter also runs on a local radio station three times a day. *Variety*'s Army Archerd, himself an institution, writes a daily column that is more trade talk and name-dropping squibs than Wicked Whispers. A publicist's job is also to feed items that keep his producer, director, and stars in these columns.

As studio publicity departments have shrunk, independent PR shops have proliferated. Press agents like Jerry Pam, Rupert Allan, Frank Liberman, and Steve Jaffe, who, with a handful of others, represent today's top talent, have merged, regrouped, and incorporated to become major firms, stressing a certain wall-to-wall carpet mentality of posh, good taste public relations. Jaffe, who recently became a partner in Gershinson, Dingilian & Associates, is about the only counterculture press agent. The youngest of the Big Timers, he handled BBS Productions publicity at the height of the *Easy Rider–Five Easy Pieces–The Last Picture Show* era, was deeply involved in the antiwar protests of his clients Jane Fonda and Donald Sutherland, and became associate producer of the John Kennedy assassination-themed *Executive Action* (leaking stories that the CIA was trying to frame the moviemakers during filming).

The unit publicist tends to develop a thick hide as he deals from an inferior position with hypersensitive egos. His loyalties are divided between the studio department chief who hired him; his stars, who after a long day on a horse in the mountains in central Arizona can think of better things to do than give interviews; the stars' press agents, who also want to have a say in publicity; and his producer, who is itching to be "creative." A Rona Jaffe junketed to the Arizona location with a *Cosmopolitan* assignment can be more spaced-out than a Paul Newman, who, while yelling "Rona, dar-ling" across dining rooms, can order the publicist to get rid of her. A David Bailey or a Douglas Kirkland out to do a *Vogue* layout on Marisa Berenson is treated like a star in his own right. Society photographers like Orlando and Dave Sutton, who plant and sell their own work on several continents and have "personal rela-tionships" with stars, are flown halfway across the world by the studio to snap staged exclusives.

It all adds up to word of mouth—"People" items in *Time*, "Newsmakers" plugs in *Newsweek*, a talk-show appearance, a Sun-day *Times* break. The sky is the limit.

Press agentry probably began with the irrepressible Harry Rei-chenbach, who, during a lull in Rudolph Valentino's career, put the Latin Lover on the front pages by persuading him to grow a beard, kept him there by reporting the protest of women and bar-bers, and capped the stunt with a public "debearding." Other clas-sics include Russell Birdwell's scouting-for-Scarlett O'Hara cam-paign for *Gone with the Wind* that went on for two hysterical years; Leo Guild's work on Paramount's *Seventeen*, which had him engi-neer the introduction of a bill in the New York state legislature to lower the legal age of consent for marriage from eighteen to seven-teen; and such silly but headline-provoking stunts as Jim Moran's literally sitting on an ostrich's egg for thirty-two days to hatch it for *The Egg and I*, or Ben Cohn's classic for *Juarez*, which involved hav-ing an underling hop into a midtown Manhattan taxi and order the driver to take him to Juarez before falling asleep in the backseat. When he woke up, the cab driver told him, "We're in Philadelphia. We ought to make Juarez, Mexico, in four days." There was an argument. Two cops jailed them both, and the story hit page one of every paper.

Contemporary ballyhoo is pretty tame. The last elaborate starlet "discovery" was Kim Novak's riding-down-Rodeo Drive-on-a-bicycle-to-be-discovered-by-Columbia-producer Louis Shurr, al-though Diane Frieson had her name changed to Dyan Cannon in the best fashion ("she's gonna make a big bang—like what? Right, like a cannon!"). Sometimes the press agents are better than the flicks they promote, namely, Twentieth Century–Fox's publicity department *casting* Rex Reed in *Myra Breckinridge*, Beverly Walker fast-talking *Esquire* into publishing the screenplay of *Two-Lane Blacktop*, or Max Bercutt orchestrating the Harvard *Lampoon* staff's not so spontaneous challenge to John Wayne to "confront" Harvard students in connection with a special screening of Warner's *McQ*. The stunt resulted in one of the biggest media breaks for a movie since Mike Todd's launching of *Around the World in 80 Days*.

To organize rapturous premieres has been standard since Sidney Grauman's days (for the 1930 opening of Howard Hughes's *Hell's Angels* at Grauman's Chinese Theater, Hollywood Boulevard was roped off for ten blocks, streetcars were detoured, and two hundred searchlights picked out thirty airplanes in the sky). Georges Cravennes masterminded the Paris world premiere of *The Longest Day* with fireworks, Allied crack troops on the Champs-Élysées, and President Charles de Gaulle and his entire cabinet in attendance (the faded art of getting presidential quotes started with Woodrow Wilson saying Griffith's *The Birth of a Nation* was "like writing history with lightning").

If putting a hit together were as easy as kidding it, every picture would be *Last Tango in Paris*, *The Godfather*, or *The Exorcist*. Even if every film is calculated to be "the one," none is foreordained to be a smash hit. The "second reality" dimension is usually accidental—cast and crews on *M*A*S*H*, *Butch Cassidy and the Sundance Kid*, and *American Graffiti* admitted after the fact that they had no inkling they were making History during the filming.

"Irony is a joke that letters play on numbers, that humanity works on demographers," *Time* wrote in a cover story analysis of the *Love Story* and return-to-romanticism phenomenon. "When the researchers decide that the nation hungers for raw meat, the country develops an appetite for Crunchy Granola; when politicians polarize, the voters cross party lines." [2]

Still, if word of mouth cannot be created by a *deus ex machina*, it can be helped along. The majors have discovered that massive, preplanned sneak previews for example can boost films that don't automatically fall into any "must see" category. After an agonizing slow start, *Sounder* was given seventy sneak previews, which Fox partially credits as being responsible for the subsequent takeoff. UA successfully sneaked *Five on the Black Hand Side*, a difficult "sell" in the untried genre of black ethnic humor. Fox repeated the formula with an unprecedented simultaneous four-hundred-theater preview, heralded by a national TV buy one week before the na-

2. *Time*, Jan. 11, 1971.

tional release of Richard Lester's *The Three Musketeers*. In an era of escalating advertising costs, sneaks have one overriding virtue. Apart from modest directory ads in local newspapers and shipping the film to the theater, they are practically costless.

The international form of sneaks and word-of-mouth building is the film festival, an institution invented by the Mussolini regime in 1932 to show off the glories of fascist Italy. There are now more than seventy full-blown international film festivals held every year—in June, a festival begins every other day. Most festivals have long since lost their innocence, but all have retained some of the intense nationalism and cultural propagandizing of that first Venice *mostra*, even if the accent has shifted from the political extreme right to the far left. To the international film community, only Cannes, with its clever mix of commerce and culture, has any dollars-and-cents meaning. The presence of 25,000 film people, 1,000 journalists, and 20 television networks makes the Cannes film festival the world's biggest annual sales convention.

Bickerings and demonstrations at the Montreal, New York, San Francisco, and Atlanta affairs, which, like Venice, refrain from awarding prizes, have been guerrilla theater for preschoolers compared to the French, Italian, and German uproars of a few years ago. It takes some imagination, even for New Left ideologues, to imagine the wrecking of the Cannes event in 1968. There was everybody who was anybody scuffling on the stage to stop the screening of Spain's official entry, Carlos Saura's *Peppermint Frappé*. Jean-Luc Godard, who with François Truffaut had called for an immediate halt to the festival on grounds of solidarity with workers and students in Paris, lost his glasses and was pitched into the chrysanthemums on the edge of the stage, while Truffaut, Roman Polanski (a jury member that year), and other *cinéastes* announced they were withdrawing their pictures and "occupying" the festival. Truffaut and Monica Vitti hung to the ends of the stage curtain to prevent it from going up, while an enormous head of Geraldine Chaplin in the opening shots of *Peppermint Frappé* was being projected on the billowing cloth. The tuxedoed audience yelled down festival director Robert Favre Le Bret with shouts of "Fascist!" when he tried to speak, and a "live" Geraldine got the mike and screamed to the projectionist to stop the film. At 5:45 P.M., after Polanski got into a tussle with Godard about who was or wasn't a Stalinist, Le Bret bowed to the inevitable and announced that "due to non-normal conditions," the festival was officially ended.

Cannes survived. The following May, the Riviera fest was back in business by throwing various fringe activities wide open ("if you can't lick 'em, join 'em") and by running more than thirty screenings a day. Day after day comatose *contestataires* and *engagé* critics staggered into the blinding sunlight asking how long it could last, while at night the chic crowd applauded films avid for destruction, revolution, and "new realities." By 1970 Cannes had grown into an untidy but exciting smash success, with the side events—Critics' Week, Directors' Fortnight, the Film Mart—growing more important than the main event. In 1971 Cannes reached its twenty-fifth anniversary, and through sheer absorption regained its pre-1968 eminence. The wheeler-dealer's Film Mart tends to overshadow the main competition, and festival gossip is less and less concerned with which film will get the *grand prix* than with what pictures are available for sale in which territory.

Berlin and Venice have been less lucky—or less cynical. The "Berlinale," always hampered by the absence of Eastern European nations (who don't recognize West Berlin as part of the Federal Republic), was wrecked by left-wing agitators in 1970—ironically with an innocent jury request about possible infringement of the festival regulation requiring all films in competition to promote international harmony, which provoked multilingual bedlam. Since then, Berlin has managed to survive as a second-rate festival, mainly because of the Bonn government's steadfast subsidy and Young Filmmakers, Third World, and other "alternative events" that bend over backward to the local ideologues. Venice, meanwhile, seems definitely killed off.

The 1970 Venice affair was a disaster, and the 1971 edition nearly didn't take place. Because Maoists said giving prizes amounted to bourgeois elitism, Venice went noncompetitive and promptly became a big bore. Although a new statute was voted by the Italian parliament in 1973, the festival was last held in 1972, and its resurrection is tied to a political agreement on policy and structure.

Moscow, which alternates on even years with the Karlovy Vary festival in Czechoslovakia, usually is a thoughtful get-together where guests and delegations from all continents enjoy each other, the juries are picturesque, and the competing films uniformly mediocre. If one year the MPAA boycotts the event because of strident anti-American propaganda movies from North Vietnam, an American delegation is back two years later. In 1973 the Brezhnev-Nixon détente had the unexpected result of moderating all criticism of the United States, and the elimination of movies, even American-made, critical of modern American society.

Such noncompetitive "repertory festivals" as New York and London introduce a worthy film or two, survey what is currently interesting on the Continent, and provide a temporary home for outcasts. The other American affairs, such as Los Angeles' Filmex, the older San Francisco festival, and the Chicago and Atlanta fests, are Chamber of Commerce events, although each has a definite personality. All festivals are heavily subsidized and most are now catering to special interests. Montreal holds a festival dedicated to films about the environment, Rheims is devoted to sports films, Trieste to science fiction, Lucca (Italy) to animation, Trento (Italy) to mountain films, and Tashkent (U.S.S.R.) to Afro-Asian cinema.

As an annual world expo, Cannes fulfills its role. It has everything: glamour, vulgarity, comic relief, melodrama, culture, money, image making, and remarkable staying power. All trends are present, from Soviet academicism and "minimal cinema" to odd, underprivileged corners of the cinema. Most professionals are there, from studio chiefs and Hollywood elder statesmen to commercial gnomes and wide-awake sexploitationers, from shell-shocked stars to the polyglot press corps always pressuring to find new faces and new sensations (while maintaining this year's occasion is the dullest on record). More than one thousand miles of film are screened for some two thousand bleary-eyed *festivaliers*, but the sheer weight of celluloid seems to disappear with one exciting movie.

Who wants his ten-million-buck epic booed by a bunch of hysterical freaks, anyway? If American industryites traditionally have felt Cannes might endanger the marketing of a film, it is now conceded that no *good* picture can be harmed by a Cannes outing. A movie that makes an impression at Cannes gets fantastic world publicity from the thousand newsmen, critics, and opinion makers who attend. Such American efforts as Jerry Schatzberg's *Panic in Needle Park* and *Scarecrow* and James Guercio's *Electra Glide in Blue* made unbeatable reputations for themselves at Cannes.

Corporate Hollywood has learned to live with it all. The American majors, who always have hefty delegations at Cannes, prefer to show their big-budget films out of competition because of the way the awards are voted, but concede the prizes are essential to keep up interest and tension during the two weeks' orgy of celluloid.

Hollywood's own Academy Awards don't create word of mouth, they sustain it. The Oscar ceremonies, which by now have established a life of their own, are a massive booster shot for the movies, a three-hour trailer for the industry and cheer for the past when Glamourland ruled supreme. The Academy race is a secret, intramural event related to excellence but rooted in economics. The votes for the winning awards are cast by the 3,000-plus members of the Academy of Motion Picture Arts and Sciences—film-craft people with a generous sprinkling of publicists and "administrators and executives." Whether the yearly April show serves truth and justice is less important to the millions of television viewers, as Richard Schickel has said, "than whether the big broadcast fulfills its implicit annual promise to turn into a psychological Le Mans with a few expensive, finely tuned egos successfully negotiating the twists and turns of the three-hour course while a satisfying number of the other entrants crash." [3]

From rather informal beginnings in 1928 in a smaller, tighter Hollywood in which the awards dinner was almost a family affair, the Oscar rituals have grown in complexity and importance. Besides the 3,000-odd stars and entertainment personalities watching "live" the now-traditional tearing of envelopes and handing of statuettes to misty-eyed ladies and quipping gentlemen, an estimated 230 million see the Oscar Night on their home screens. The show is seen live in Canada, Mexico, Brazil, and Australia, and delayed telecasts are presented in Great Britain and eight other countries.

Now totally underwritten by television, the Oscars are not only a vote of confidence in the way we were, they are also cold cash in boxoffice tills.

Nominations alone mean additional playdates for a film, possibly at more favorable rental terms than it had the first time out, and more business and longer runs. The Oscars themselves don't all carry equal weight, but the importance of more than one increases exponentially. A million dollars has been the figure the industry

3. *Time*, Apr. 15, 1974.

guesses the Oscar is worth to a movie, but for a big picture a million is a rather conservative figure. The Oscar can well mean the difference between profit and loss. *Darling* and *The Pawnbroker* were unquestionably helped by the Oscars, and *A Man for All Seasons* had more reason to be grateful than *The Godfather* or *The Sound of Music*, which were doing fine without the nine-inch statuettes.

The stakes are high, and studios accuse one another—always covertly—of trying to influence the votes of employees. The suggestion is that the majors enjoy a sort of sweetheart contract with labor here and that wage-earning Academy members can be pressured to put their ballots where their butter is. The pressure exists without anyone having to exert it. A major film takes months to shoot, and such long togetherness of working, eating, and often living under one location roof thousands of miles from home naturally makes the cast and crew of one hundred-odd members form personal loyalties which are likely to be remembered during the annual spring rites.

Unlike Cannes and other festivals with their VIP juries, the Oscar has undeniably democratic voting. There is, however, a lingering major-studio bias and the cliquishness of the "branch voting"—art directors voting on art directing, editors on editing, actors on acting, and *everybody* on "best picture." While maintaining it is logical that specialists judge specialists, the Academy has given in to various reforms, although at a snail's pace. In an attempt to bring the profile closer in line with the industry as it works today, the Academy demoted 300 members to nonvoting status in 1970.

Stronger reforms are always suggested. Rod Steiger would like to have the previous years' winners vote for the following year's nominations, and there has been talk of a final selection committee (there is no proof that any of the members actually *see* the films for which they cast ballots). The most striking proposal has been Karl Malden's idea that Oscar Night be turned into a bands-playing, delegates-shouting, convention-inspired electioneering free-for-all, with actors getting on the stump and giving "the man who" speeches.

Perhaps democratic processes cannot be applied to the arts to the satisfaction of any majority. Ideally, the Oscars recognize achievements among fellows. At worst, they are an indigenous form of idol worship, or Hollywood's particular piece of cultural imperialism. "The evening becomes as complicated as a good movie, with great splashes of splendor and also intimations of the passing nature of earthly kingdoms," Charles Champlin, entertainment editor of the Oscars' hometown paper, *The Los Angeles Times*, has reflected. "There is a split-level sense of how little the night matters, and how much." [4]

A split-level feeling that can be expanded, at a higher level of abstraction, to cover the cinema as a whole.

4. *Los Angeles Times*, Mar. 25, 1973.

12

Producers and Other Vices

IF ANYBODY "INVENTED" the producer it was Thomas H. Ince, a director who became too successful. Ince began working for American Biograph in 1910 and by 1914 was as famous as D. W. Griffith. A major force in the blossoming industry, he soon owned his own palatial studio in Culver City. When he found himself devoting far more time to organizing his studio than to actual directing, he began hiring "production managers," who worked with him and the scenario writers on the preparation of the plot lines. When completed a scenario was rubber-stamped, "Shoot as written."

The position of the producer has always been baffling, and Hollywood lore is full of unkind stories about him. The producer started as a business representative and jockeyed himself into creative control to end up, sixty years after Ince invented him, as a deal maker. A producer has been defined as an executive who wears a worried look on his assistant's face and, during the golden era of nepotism, as someone who produces only relatives.

"Let us get the firing squads into the studios and as humanely as possible rid ourselves of the average producer with his average public reaction to the average boxoffice success," British director Bryan Forbes wrote in 1964.[1] "Who, alas, needs him? He generates about as much artistic excitement as a sackful of dead mice and the total sum of his cinematic knowhow is his ability to read the balance sheet of his last picture."

1. *Show*, Apr. 1964.

Five years earlier, Hollywood's bitter historian, Ezra Goodman, summed up the traditional producer as someone who "does not write, does not direct, does not photograph, does not even dress the sets or do the leading lady's hair." [2] Ben Hecht was perhaps crueler. "Writers and directors can be carried away by a 'strange' characterization or a new point of view; a producer, never," Hecht wrote in his memoirs. "I discovered early in my movie work that a movie is never better than the stupidest man connected with it. There are times when this distinction may be given to the writer or director. Most often it belongs to the producer." [3]

In 1974, *New Yorker* critic Pauline Kael invited directors "to break out of this humiliating suicidal struggle with the entrepreneurs," the executives, producers, and agents. "If the directors started one distribution company or several . . . they might have to spend time on business problems, but much less time on deal-making sessions, those traumatic meetings at which the businessmen air their grievances while the artists anxiously vulgarize the projects they're submitting, hoping to make them sound commerical enough." [4]

If all thirties and forties producers have long since sunk without trace, Irving Thalberg has remained as the archetype of the species. Possessing a canny knowledge of what would please the public plus a knack for developing stars and doctoring scripts, Thalberg was head of production at Universal at the age of twenty and, under Louis B. Mayer, turned MGM into the greatest film factory. He brought the preview to a ritualistic and ruthless perfection. All films were dry-run, returned for re-editing or even reshooting, and previewed again until audiences in outlying Los Angeles areas laughed or cried on cue. Thalberg, who furnished F. Scott Fitzgerald with the material for the hero of *The Last Tycoon*, died at the age of thirty-seven, to be enshrined as the classical *wunderkind* (an Academy Award bestowed irregularly on assertedly worthy industryites is named after him) and to appear to posterity as a somewhat absurd example of middle-period baroque.

During the peak of the fabulous twenties and thirties, the majors commanded armies of producers, directors, and stars. A studio

2. Ezra Goodman, *The Fifty-Year Decline and Fall of Hollywood*. New York: Simon & Schuster, 1961.
3. Ben Hecht, *A Child of the Century*. New York: Simon & Schuster, 1965.
4. *New Yorker*, Aug. 5, 1974.

taught, groomed, and managed new faces with the efficiency of prime rib stock breeders; they molded and manipulated the careers of stars whose names are still household words. If boxoffice returns justified a thrust in a certain direction, the studio chiefs had at their fingertips the pool of writers, directors, and stars to put the hunch on film. Although Thalberg was often wrong in his estimates of trends—he felt talkies would never catch on and took longer than most to realize the stage was a poor source for screen material—he was the first administrator with a craving for "creativity," a precedent David Selznick in particular would carry to Byzantine heights with pathological interference in the pictures he produced.

The producer is still here, but the profession as well as the *kind* of person acceding to producership have changed radically. The contract system faded when television and the antitrust decrees dismembering the production-distribution combines caused the studios to decimate their stables of players, writers, and technical personnel, and everybody became a free-lancer. But talent agents had to find work for their clients, if they were not to become vast unemployment agencies. In self-defense, they seized the initiative, and in the early 1950s the era of the packager was born. Jules Stein and Lew Wasserman of MCA carried packaging to its ultimate conclusion by moving into production, first with MCA's Revue production division and later by purchasing Universal Pictures and Decca Records. In 1962 the justice department forced MCA to choose between agenting and production. MCA pulled out of the agency business. Its nearest rival, William Morris, also moved toward production, playing an active role in forming the original Four-Star TV production company, but elected to remain an agency.

A producer is, almost by definition, a person in transit, which may explain the turnover of names on contemporary credit crawls. In 1970 the Producers' Guild calculated that of 116 producers, executive producers, and associate producers listed on fifty-nine films in production, only 18 had credits going back more than four years. If a producer has a hot property and a hot concept, he can wheel and deal. If his package is worth anything to the majors and they like his ingredients, he can make almost any deal he wants within the economics of a given year. The next year, however, it's a new ballgame. Of sixty-one features in preparation or being shot in January 1974, four were being produced by their own directors, seventeen by producers with recognizable names and previous credits, and forty by newcomers. With Hal Wallis in knighted retirement in Britain and Ross Hunter tiptoeing in and out of TV production, Richard Zanuck, Paul Monash, M. J. (Mike) Frankovich, Ray Stark, Howard Koch, the James Bond duo Albert Broccoli and Harry Saltzman, and perhaps Walter Mirisch are the last active producers with careers stretching back ten years. Robert Evans and David Picker are a pair of former executives who, like Frankovich, have left front offices for so-called independent production—so-called since Evans' output is automatically Paramount–financed and released and Picker's is a UA product. Philip d'Antoni and Alan J. Pakula are a pair of producers who have carried their creative urge to the logical conclusion and become directors.

The days of the Mike Todds, Sam Spiegels, and even former press agents like Arthur P. Jacobs have ended for a number of reasons. Even discounting the dominance of the director, the professional designation "producer" has lost its meaning. A skilled packager-agent can elevate himself to producer without benefit of, or interest in, production experience. The majors need these deal makers and are quite liberal with the title ("executive producer" has never meant anything) in exchange for a hot property.

The pattern of studio reliance on a mixed bag of project sources instead of "in-house" development of properties has been standard for years at United Artists. Lately the practice has spread to Universal, Paramount, Columbia, Warner's, and Fox, and, as such, perpetuates the role of the producer-packager.

The majority of today's producers are agents and lawyers, and their background in film production is usually so limited that they cannot intervene once a picture is rolling (although at sneak-preview time they again turn into the self-styled experts they were when the picture was being packaged). If they are not upgraded agents, they are likely to be friends or relatives of big-name stars, émigrés from TV or Broadway (where audience tastes differ sharply from those of filmgoers), or chief accountants. According to Brut Production chief George Barrie, the downward trend in film attendance may be attributed to their overwhelming bad taste.

"Instead of lawyers, accountants, and real estate experts, who have been elevated to creative decision making, the industry will have to have the kind of men and women who are essentially filmmakers with good taste and overall skills," Barrie has said. "The independent producer simply represents another slice of the pie in dividing up profits and, more importantly, creative control."

Barrie feels the producers exist because many writers and directors have abdicated the packaging of their work.

If the director as superstar so far has failed to translate into box-office consistency, the erosion of the producer's instinct and persistence is even more glaring. Of 170 new films earning domestic rentals of $4 million or more between 1968 and 1972, only eight producers could lay claim to three or more of these pictures, *Variety* concluded. Thirty years earlier, the number of producers contributing at least three of the top grossers was twenty-three. On *Variety*'s 1974 all-time boxoffice champions list, only the James Bond–wave producers Broccoli and Saltzman appeared more than twice, whereas Robert Wise, George Roy Hill, David Lean, Stanley Kubrick, Peter Bogdanovich, Mike Nichols, and (Bond-director) Guy Hamilton directed three each of the top one hundred moneymaking films.

Telltale indications of the producer's waning power are that he cannot package without a director (the first question studio executives ask after being handed a property is, "Who's going to direct it?") and that studio chiefs tend to bypass him in vital production decisions. Yet a producer can be extremely valuable. A "working producer"—to distinguish him from the deal maker—is a good administrator who understand figures, can deal with people on all levels, and knows how to smooth out angles. In an ideal producer-director relationship, he is also someone whose judgment the filmmaker trusts, a failsafe mechanism that is tripped when, in the creative fury, the director may be so involved with individual trees that he loses sight of the forest.

Production fees are still handsome. Robert Chartoff and Irwin Winkler, who during the last few years have produced an average of one picture every four months, earn $100,000 per film. Their "fee" comes off the top of the budget.

"A good producer today is someone who can recognize a good story and who can back his taste with money," says Winkler. "It doesn't have to be fantastic sums, but *some* money has to be put up, otherwise everything remains talk, talk, talk. He is also someone who knows how to supervise—discreetly; money must be controlled. Finally, he is someone who knows whether to blow the whole publicity budget on TV spots or buy page 3 of next Sunday's entertainment sections all over the country."

Chartoff, a former lawyer who met Winkler in the offices of the William Morris Agency in 1964, believes that the ideal movie is a project uniting people who, when rubbed together, produce sparks. "What we're interested in is source material—original scripts, books, plays, unpublished manuscripts, forgotten screenplays— that captivates contemporary imagination and has dramatic impact."

Chartoff and Winkler sell their packages to anyone. Explains Chartoff: "We go to, say, Warner's, and say, 'Look, we have such and such a project that so and so is interested in directing and so and so wants to star in; the whole thing can be made for so and so much money.' United Artists, Columbia, or any other of the majors then looks at it and says yes or no, sometimes no because ours happens to be a western and they have twelve other westerns sitting. Or yes, if we can bring it down to such and such a figure."

"We haven't managed to get Tom Stoppard's *Rosencrantz and Guildenstern Are Dead* off the ground despite interest by both John Boorman and Joseph Losey," Winkler said during the filming of *Fat Chance*. "The excuse was that it's a costume picture and, as such, boxoffice poison." Other packages that haven't come together for Chartoff and Winkler include Kurt Vonnegut's *Mother Night*, a pop spy yarn that has some of the blackest humor and best plotting of any Vonnegut novel, and *Something Wicked This Way Comes*, the most nightmarish of Ray Bradbury's science fiction, which Sam Peckinpah was to have directed.

To fall in line with what they see as the new reality, the two partners want to slow down to two pictures a year. "Films live longer," says Winkler. "Little pictures and even not-so-bad ones are dead. It's ironic, but the new interest in film has a tendency to eliminate, not to encourage, young filmmakers' first efforts. Everybody wants big, beautiful, and meaningful movies. That means *A Clockwork Orange* can stay around for years, which means people will go less to the movies. Movie buffs have to realize that a consequence of more significant films is less popular films."

If producers, as guardians against the unusual, the profane, and the crazy, are responsible for a safe sameness of American films that, as Barrie says, has helped depress movie attendance, Hollywood's unions are guilty of a myopic backwardness that has been just as deadening.

Every advance has been a battle against vested labor interests. Grips resented lightweight xenon lights giving off more illumination than 285-pound brute lights, and soundmen fought portable quarter-inch recorders. Cinemobile's founder, Fouad Said, had to scrub advertising showing that his piggybacking studios on wheels could also be airlifted in cargo planes because unions felt such mobility encouraged runaway filming abroad, and the first attempt at shooting features on videotape was literally run out of town in 1965. If every other American home doesn't yet have a videocassette player hooked into the living room TV set, the reason is a union pie-in-the-sky attitude and not lack of technological breakthrough (see Chapter 14). Union demands can go to absurd lengths: one of the Writers' Guild of America contract demands in 1973 was that two telephone discussions between a writer and a producer actually constituted a preliminary agreement.

Union leaders are faced not only with a general deregimentation of moviemaking, but also with the growing amateurization of memberships. Only 5 percent of the huge Screen Actors' Guild (SAG) members are professionals, i.e., earn more than $8,000 a year acting. At negotiation time with the Association of Motion Picture and Television Producers, the majority of the membership doesn't mind voting for a strike action that will not only paralyze feature production but throw off a year's TV programming.

Hollywood labor was not always the most reactionary element of the industry. The first attempts at organizing film workers only lacked company goon squads to compare with the birth pangs of the United Auto Workers. The Academy of Motion Picture Arts and Sciences, which, today, is mainly devoted to bestowing Oscars, was originally a union-busting maneuver and, as such, succeeded in obstructing unionizing efforts by Actors' Equity by becoming the group spokesman for actors and by preempting the functions of an incipient writers' guild. A refusal by stagehands to go along with a 50 percent salary cut led to a strike in 1933, the first of a series of convulsive strike-lockouts over unionizing. Always ambivalent about money, the 1930s writing colony was by far the most progressive force in Glamourland, attacking poverty and social injustice in a surprising number of scripts and embracing the Rooseveltian New Deal, if not outright socialism, as a matter of course (the House Un-American Activities Committee was to remember the prewar radical chic, the rallies for Republican Spain, the near-underground organizing of the Screen Writers' Guild, and the Federal Theater and Writers' Project when it decided to conduct "an investigation of Communism in motion pictures" in 1948).

The chipping away, if not breaking down, of rigid unionism has aired out and liberated the medium (it is now possible to move a chair without being a member of the stagehands' local, although a cinematographer still cannot be his own camera operator), but it has also killed apprenticeship.

Six hundred and thirteen American schools offer 5,889 classes in film and television, and 22,466 students are enrolled in these courses. One hundred and ninety-four schools offer degrees, either in film and/or TV, or, with majors in film and/or TV, degrees in a related field. According to a survey by the American Film Institute, the majority of these schools rate film production as the most important aspect, with film history/criticism a close second, and "education media" third. Professionals who have visited or lectured at such cinematic A-1 campuses as UCLA and USC in Hollywood's own backyard have come away appalled by the cinema departments' lack of touch with reality. By no stretch of the imagination can these courses be said to be training grounds for work in the film industry.

To reunite key talent and technicians for postproduction work has become a skyrocketing proposition. "Everybody lives in Boulder, Colorado, or New York, or Sundance, Utah," says producer Arnold Orgolini. "The moment the last shot is in the can, the star gets into his Lear jet and the key grip into his camper. Everybody is just off." In 1974 Jon Voight was flown 12,000 miles round-trip from the filming of *The Odessa File* in Munich to loop three words in *Conrack* at Twentieth Century–Fox.

The advantage of the current state of affairs is that a "wide open" industry looking for new ideas offers chances for interesting people to work. "I think there is a great deal more freedom today and we're just getting there," says Orgolini. "Ironically, more opportunities are also showing the glaring lack of good filmmakers available."

13

Discreet Qualms of the Bourgeoisie

SEXUAL FREEDOM in Denmark is not only the title of a late 1960s semisoft Camembert, it is also a state of mind that American filmgoers probably will never enjoy. An overview of the last decade may look like one long retreat for law-and-order forces, but that doesn't mean it is only a matter of time before adult Americans can join the erotic frontier of screen freedom.

And who says so?

America's leading pornographers.

Americans are not congenitally more strait-laced than Danes, say the porn-house owners—there are simply vested interests working against any total liberation of the screen. Lobbies of citizens for decent literature employ $40,000-a-year lawyers, says hard-core entrepreneur Vince Miranda. Porn exhibitors defend themselves with scores of other attorneys. Anti-smut campaigns are Pavlovian reflexes of nearly anyone running for public office, and busting a movie theater is so much easier for a policeman than apprehending burglars and muggers. Why, the movie house is right there and even advertises when it changes its playbill.

David Friedman, a Cornell University graduate who has made such items as *Trader Hornee* and *Thar She Blows* and has financial interests in twenty-eight porn theaters from Atlanta to Seattle, says pornography is its own diminishing returns. And it is true that hard-core does chase soft-core off the screens, but these types of material also create habits. Pornographically speaking, New York is its own scene, Washington is a "solid gold" hard-core city, and the greater L.A. bedroom communities are the only situation where soft- and hard-core can live side by side. As owner of a thirty-cinema California chain and producer of *Diamond Stud* and *American Sexual Revolution*, Miranda had forty-four police actions against his theaters in 1973 alone and has been the defendant in a *Deep Throat* court case in Beverly Hills that ran through hung jury and second trial.

Deep Throat was made by Gerard Damiano, also the creator of the erotic psychodrama *The Devil in Miss Jones*. A stocky, bearded New Yorker, Damiano was a hairdresser in Queens until 1967 when he sold a beauty salon and a wig store and began making soft-core. "People make sex films because they want to make films," he says. "Sex films now are to moviemakers what the Borscht circuit was to comedians—the only place you can learn outside the restrictive unions. It's the best schooling."

Damiano began with sex manual–type films, bogus documentaries with on-screen sex but always with a doctor telling the audience that this could help the viewers' marriages. "In *Sex U.S.A.*, we gave them the old socially redeeming values, but by the time of *Deep Throat* I had decided to do what I liked," Damiano told *Playboy* in 1973. "How can you convince people that what you're doing is legit if you don't believe in it yourself?" [1]

Since *Deep Throat*, made for $40,000 and drawing $1.3 million during its first thirty-nine weeks in Manhattan alone, Damiano has tried his hand at straight movemaking and has become a client of the William Morris Agency. His star, Linda Lovelace, has also tried fully-clothed showbiz, as have the two other porn queens. Marilyn Chambers, the Ivory Snow box girl who starred in *Behind the Green Door*, has tried a nightclub act, and Tina Russell, of *Just Another Woman* fame, has recorded an album of comic quips.

The Los Angeles police department considers its city to be the hard-core capital of the world (although *Deep Throat* was shot in Miami), with San Francisco the number two production center. Elaborate porn flicks cost upwards of $30,000, require three weeks' preparation and one week's shooting, and pay their actors $150 to $200 a day and their crews $250 a week. "A hard-core film today is as strictly constructed as a medieval morality play," says Friedman, acknowledging that business in America's estimated 730 porn

1. *Playboy*, Aug. 1973.

houses declines steadily. "There are just so many positions you can film."

The absence of national guidelines in pornography since the Supreme Court decision on obscenity in 1973 has made the pressure against the porn distributors and exhibitors relentless. In 1973 an exasperated judge gave a Texas theater owner eighteen years in jail for showing a dirty movie, a sentence everybody knew was senseless and probably would be squashed in appeal. Indeed, the costs of fighting obscenity charges in courts around the country were cited as one of the reasons New York's Sherpix, Inc., went out of business in 1974. The company, which hit it big in 1970 with *The Stewardesses* (rentals $6.8 million) and for several years was the top distributor of "class" hard-core, acknowledged its legal costs had been extraordinary. The final straw for Sherpix came with a conviction on federal obscenity charges in Washington for showing *Hot Circuit*. It was the second trial in the matter, the first having ended in a hung jury.

Pornographers are banded together in the Adult Film Association (AFAA) under the presidency of Friedman. Unlike the none-too-brave Motion Picture Association of America (MPAA), the AFAA is pushing for state-by-state legislation to permit adults to see any film they want.

Local versus national definitions of obscenity are at the center of current legalistic hairsplitting. After more than a decade of liberalizing verdicts, the U.S. Supreme Court reversed itself in 1973 and declared that there is no longer a national standard for obscenity—that each community, through its judges and juries—can best determine what is obscene. Effectively engendered by President Nixon's appointment of four of the five justices who voted as a majority, the Court's ruling failed to define what it meant by a community and also left unclear whether its ruling was aimed at hardcore or whether serious works that offended local sensibilities could be banned. "It is neither realistic nor constitutionally sound to read the First Amendment as requiring that the people of Maine or Mississippi accept public depiction of conduct found tolerable in Las Vegas or New York," Chief Justice Warren Burger wrote for the majority.[2] The ruling, however, skirted the issue. If one state,

2. A 1974 survey of Kansas City residents by Research Associates showed 65 percent of that midwest city's population agreed that adults have the right to view any picture of actual

county, city, or borough is allowed to suppress a film, novel, or other form of expression because that state, county, city or borough finds it obsence, its ban is allowed because the First Amendment does *not* protect it. Another state, county, city, or borough might not find it objectionable, meaning that the First Amendment cannot be interpreted to protect freedom of the press in one state and not in another.

Two weeks after the ruling, the Georgia Supreme Court upheld a local ruling that Mike Nichols' *Carnal Knowledge* was obscene. The decision caused a stir in Hollywood and provoked the MPAA to appeal the ruling in the hope that the justices would, if not reverse themselves, at least spell out what is and what is not obscene. When the Supreme Court did rule in June 1974, it overturned the conviction of the Georgia theater manager who had shown *Carnal Knowledge*. The justices, however, were still split on the basic strategy for dealing with obscenity. Justice William Brennan, who feels that government would do better to abandon the field altogether, filed a brief opinion gloomily noting that the court had once again fallen back into "the mire of case-by-case determinations of obscenity." Some publishers and movie officials felt the decision might help force porn-hunting prosecutors to distinguish between hard and soft, but Playboy Enterprises' Robert Gutwillig complained that the *Carnal Knowledge* ruling said: we don't know what pornography is, but we'll know if we see it.

"They should have taken their thesis a step farther," commented director Arthur Hiller ingeniously. "Not only does each community have different standards, but *each individual* has different standards, and each individual should have the right to decide what it is he wants to see, read, or hear."

In the meantime, the AFAA has started an ingenious suit of its own which, in effect, would overturn all federal obscenity laws for failing to meet the high court's new criteria. If the Supreme Court, the argument goes, reached its 1973 decision because it found that national standards, if they existed, were unascertainable and unprovable, then federal obscenity cases are determined by nonexistent guidelines, a clear case of denial of due process of law.

If Damiano's *Deep Throat* was the first porn movie to become a

or simulated sex acts in films and magazines, while 21 percent disagreed and 14 percent had no opinion.

cultural event, the permissive age began for the movies in 1966—a year before Denmark abolished film censorship for adults—when the Supreme Court declared precensorship unconstitutional and put an end to the last municipal censorship boards (in Baltimore and Chicago).

The industry has never waited for the high court to protect it from bluenoses and has very effectively fought off legislation at *any* level of government for nearly fifty years. When 1920s stars began believing their own publicity and behaving as kings and queens who could do no wrong, and a series of scandals outraged the public and provoked a protest that assumed the form of a threatened national censorship, Hollywood decided to regulate itself.

The studio moguls got together and appointed Will H. Hays, a Presbyterian elder and postmaster general in the Harding administration, as overseer and "czar" of movie morals. By creating ground rules and enforcing them, Hays averted national censorship—and, considered even more nightmarish, a morass of conflicting state, county, city, and borough bluenose laws. Although the Hays rules, or Production Code, further standardized plots and screenfare (virtue was *always* rewarded, sin *always* punished), it worked with various revisions for thirty-six years.

The old handbook of proprieties for the screen was scrapped in 1968, long after Americans discovered that married couples sleep in double beds rather than the twin beds the Code had insisted on for so long. This and other specific strictures had made the Production Code seem foolish, limiting, and irrelevant, but the nonlegal ratings system, which the MPAA imported from England to replace the yes-or-no Code was a cosmetic compromise that the industry itself soon began to shoot holes in. Shifting the responsibility for what young people can see from the theater manager, the distributor, and the filmmaker to the parents, the system's categories of G, GP, R, and X (an M classification, for mature audiences, was soon dropped) fixed any and all films on a sliding moral scale. As MPAA president Jack Valenti repeats *ad nauseam*, the rating system is made for parents, not professional critics, movie historians, or anyone else over seventeen.

"I cannot understand why there is so much savagery leaping from the pens of some film critics about the ratings," Valenti wrote in a reply to *New York Times* critic Vincent Canby's suggestion that the system be scrapped. "It is as if they are void in knowledge about what happens in the real world of film in countries all over the globe. There are only two countries on earth today in which governments do not control, or monitor, films. One of these free-film nations is the U.S.A. We want to keep it that way. (Legal fact: the Supreme Court has already decided that children have lesser First Amendment rights than adults. Perhaps we need to conduct a legal seminar for angry ratings-system critics)." [3]

Valenti's point would be unassailable if MPAA member companies hadn't managed to fish around in the alphabet soup for softer letters for some of their expensive endeavors—MGM's *Ryan's Daughter* and Warner's *The Exorcist* are prime examples—if Valenti hadn't tried so hard to dissociate MPAA companies from the pornographers by proposing "model legislation" to, in effect, create double standards about the X, and if all this (plus the newspapers' "ghettoizing" of, if not outright ban on, X-rated advertising) hadn't made the rating system into something more than a convenient shopper's guide for parents.

Reprobation is always a matter of place and time, and defining obscenity has eluded the best legal minds for centuries. But can only sex be obscene?

Much more irritating for the industry because it raises questions about community responsibility is violence and the entirely modern phenomenon of *beautiful* violence on the screen.

The sixties were shocked by violence. This decade was, in hind-sight, a romantic decade of dissent and confrontation but energized with hope and discovery. The American bedrock shivered with so many quakes that violent screen fantasies finally caused a public outcry (fear of congressional wrath after a report to the surgeon general established a link between televised violence and aggressive behavior even in normal children had networks crack down on TV mayhem for a while). The post-Vietnam, post-Watergate seventies have produced a numbness to pain and corruption that has rubbed off on the screen.

If Terence Young's *From Russia with Love* in 1963 was the first James Bond picture to treat its subject as a stylish fantasy (in *Dr. No*, sex-and-sadism was still tentative and killings were not yet dissociated from pain), Ralph Nelson's 1966 *Duel at Diablo* was the first to *show* an arrow enter the flesh, while a year later Robert Aldrich gave audiences a half-hour high of slaughter in *The Dirty*

3. *New York Times*, June 18, 1972.

Dozen. The "landmark," however, was Sam Peckinpah's *The Wild Bunch* in 1969, which contributed new delights to the spectacle of death with its elegiac slow-motion slaughter. Meanwhile, spaghetti westerns stripped the genre of the morality-play dimension, the Marshall Dillon–John Wayne figure riding out to put an end to loonies at the fringe of society abusing their guns. Contemporary westerns—Italian or homespun—and urban cops'n robbers formula flicks have totally eliminated "good guys," insofar as both sides line up malicious, vengeful, and morally demented characters, if not stylish sadists, who all commit the same number of mutilations, beatings, acid-tossing, and killings.

By the time of Peckinpah's *Straw Dogs*, audiences were supposed to accept violence as a sensual pleasure, and in Mark Rydell's GP-rated *The Cowboys*, John Wayne's murder is avenged by a group of children who torture one rustler and end up killing every member of the supporting cast. Only one film has ever been rated X for violence—*I Drink Your Blood*—and that was changed to an R when cuts were made.

"There seems to be an assumption that if you're offended by movie brutality, you are somehow playing into the hands of the people who want censorship," Pauline Kael wrote in reviewing *A Clockwork Orange*. "Actually, those who believe in censorship are primarily concerned with sex and they generally worry about violence only when it's eroticized. This means that practically no one raises the issue of the possible cumulative effects of movie brutality." [4] When *Newsweek*'s Peter Morgenstern put the question of violence and ratings to Valenti in 1972, the MPAA president said ratings were doing what they were supposed to—marking certain pictures off-limits to children and warning parents that certain other films might be unsuitable for minors. "I don't think it's the rating system that's in collapse," Valenti said. "It may be that parents just don't care any more." [5] A nationwide *Newsweek* survey of theater operators revealed little or no public dissatisfaction with the ratings or the violence of new movies.

The Vietnam war, the explosion of street crime and of government intrigue at the highest level, seem to mock middle-class gentility and to make despair and cynicism more than fashionable. More than ever modern heroic acts seem to be possible only as schemes of fools and lunatics. Makers of formula entertainment mine new

4. *New Yorker*, Jan. 1, 1972.
5. *Newsweek*, Feb. 14, 1972.

veins of popular moods and come up with screenfare that accepts corruption and sentimentalizes defeat. In such films as *The Seven Ups*, *Magnum Force*, and *Death Wish*, mayhem has become even more senseless than in earlier potboilers, and their lawmen heroes no longer bring evildoers to justice—they *are* justice, implying that the "system" is rotting, anyway, and that cops are not better people but just more effective than the varmints they track down. Commenting on Ted Post's R-rated *Magnum Force*, Miss Kael could write that what is alarming is the emotionlessness of so many violent movies, "not the rare violent movies (*Bonnie and Clyde*, *The Godfather*, *Mean Streets*) that make us care about the characters and what happens to them. . . . The movie is full of what in a moral landscape would be sickening scenes of death: a huge metal girder smashed right into a man's face, and the audience is meant not to empathize and to hide from the sight but to say 'Wow!' " [6]

The report to the surgeon general notwithstanding, sociologists tend to agree that modern society has no identifiable community standards (essentially a lawyer's term, they say), because attitudes and modes are too dissimilar, if not outright polarized, for meaningful morals legislation. While many don't see any imminent disaster in audiences grooving on ultraviolence, they feel there must be outer limits to sexual explicitness on the screen. They feel that literary pornography is somewhat more tolerable, because filmed (and staged) sex involves others—the people *doing* it and the people watching, perhaps watching us watch—which amounts to a tremendous breach of individual privacy.

Proponents of total freedom on the screen talk about such positive results as feeling genuinely closer to their fellows, less puzzled and less afraid of them, more aware of bodies and of the emotions they have had in common after emerging from screenings. Their "higher" argument is that carrying the notion of protecting children and immature minds to the point where *all* social standards are consistently adapted to the youngest and weakest member of society would lead to an even more intolerable state of affairs.

Both arguments skirt the issue of filmmakers' responsibility. "At least two sets of signals are operating here, and the confusion between them raises some anguishing questions that no one knows how to answer," Morgenstern concluded in *Newsweek*'s survey on violence. "Where does an artist's responsibility end? With the truthful depiction of his personal vision, or with its social effects?"

6. *New Yorker*, Jan. 14, 1974.

14

Blurred Frontiers

INCREASINGLY, the distinction between cinema and television is a question of different mental landscapes. The *technical* gap between them is constantly narrowing. Big-screen movies are shot on video-tape, and in a few years videocassettes or, more likely, videodiscs promise to have us all at home playing our favorite reel of *Casablanca* on our television set. Before the end of the decade, the very notion of projected images and sound will be fused into "audiovision" (AV), and AV will be a household word and product.

In the Hollywood industry, the revolution is already sinking in, although its impact has not yet been felt in music, theater, publishing, and journalism, which will all be affected, if not totally transformed, by the onrushing all-media technology.

A society fast fragmenting at the level of values and life-styles, we are told, demands a corresponding diversity in art, entertainment, education, and "psychiatric services." Tomorrow will be a world of overchoice, of a surfeit of subcults. In the postindustrial era, human needs will tend to shift from materialism toward a desire for self-realization. After providing material satisfaction, technological societies must concern themselves with spiritual gratification. As we move from homogeneity to heterogeneity, mass communications are "de-massified."

The godfathers standing over the newborn videocassette in 1970 were as many as their predictions were optimistic. The videocassette, according to them, will act as a dramatic transformer of cultural habits. Hollywood will again become boomtown; indeed the entire entertainment industry—if that is what we should continue to call it—will know untold prosperity. Going a step further, video is director Alexandre Astruc's dream of the "camera pen" come true—filmmaking mechanically as simple as writing. Better still, video will finally free the movies from the overpowering economic straightjacket. "Think publishing," is the advice of some video enthusiasts. "No almighty industry, no studios, but a group of cartridge manufacturers, 'publishing,' quite mechanically, individual works." Video is cheap. Video is not photochemicals, but electronics; everything is instant. Prime-time television series seen by 20 million viewers are canceled as losers, but an opera, for example—shot on video and "canned" in a cassette that snaps into a TV set—only needs to attract 500,000 patrons at $20 each to earn back its cost, and *that* is what the revolution is about.

The cinema no longer caters to a single, faceless mass audience. The commercial-versus-art-house dualism has already fragmented and probably will continue to shatter the medium into ever-varying ranges of subjects and treatments catering to ever-specializing audiences. Videodiscs will be the real audience-splitter, and as such will be the equivalent of the paperback in publishing.

The videocassette, said *Time*, will quicken the already bewildering pace of life by carrying the arts, education, and cultural tastes yet further from any established norm.[1] Marshall McLuhan was characterically more sweeping: "The videocassette will affect every aspect of our lives; will give us new needs, goals, and desires, and will upset all political, educational, and commercial establishments." In *Future Shock*, Alvin Toffler said that the social thrust toward diversity and increased individual choice "affects our mental as well as our material surroundings" and that television was the last medium still "homogenizing taste."

Now, a few years after that book appeared, when resource limitations and energy shortfalls seem to make parsimonious, not prodigal, attitudes the way of tomorrow, the aggressive future-shock rhetoric has a slightly naive aftertaste. Nevertheless, the Third Revolution—the first two waves of the electronic age were radio and television—hasn't gone away, and "postcinematic" audiovision *is* approaching. Once again, the death sentence of cinema as we

1. *Time*, Aug. 10, 1970.

know it has been pronounced, in harsher, no-nonsense terms, and its rebirth in electronics foretold. The assault is now two-pronged, coming both fore and aft, so to speak—in the basic stuff movies are made on and in the way in which we see the end-result.

At first. A few years after euphoria, sober reevaluation, and discreet pullback, the videocassette has surfaced again. Recorders and players are being turned out—and sold by the tens of thousands in the United States, Europe, and Japan. Most of the hardware is going to commercial markets: industries needing audiovisual teaching aids, ships, apartment complexes, and hotels. After pilot projects in New York and Toronto, trade names such as Pik-a Movie (Fox, Zeiss-Ikon), Hotelevision (Columbia, Rediffusion Ltd., Rank), and Computer Television (Time, Inc., EMI) popped up in chain hotels in North America and Europe.

At first, the only problem seemed to be a profusion of systems. Like the movies before the 35-mm., four-sprockets-per-frame standardization of 1889, the video-cartridge world was a disconcerting if joyous confusion. A Sony cassette could not snap into an Avco or Colorvision player, nor could an Electronic Video Recording (EVR) player accommodate a Selecta-Vision spool, and by 1972 RCA Corporation, Columbia Broadcasting System (CBS), and Avco had pulled out of the hardware race, leaving the more sophisticated "second generation" Disco-Vision, owned by MCA, and Philips' VCR process the likeliest winners in the ultimate battle of systems, especially since both could be meshed with each other. To strengthen their lead in the multimillion-dollar sweepstakes, Philips and MCA decided in 1974 to join forces, with Philips manufacturing the home players and MCA concentrating on the "software," the videodisk and the programming.

What will be the new medium's message? Pop festivals of *Hamlet*, Broadway musicals, symphony concerts, highlights of the World Cup, or "how to" series on cooking and sex? Or *War and Peace* unabridged (not running two or six hours, but sixty hours, or whatever it takes)? Or will the pressures of competing systems inevitably lead to mass-market conformism and "coffee table" culture?

When MCA launched its sophisticated laser-principle Disco-Vision—*all* trade names seem to be inelegant—Lew Wasserman's brain trust decided that its software would simply be the entire backlog of Universal pictures. MCA thought the electronic poker game through to some sort of realistic conclusion by deciding that there will be no vast and complicated rental marketing system, that the discs will be sold outright, and to hell with copyrights.

Talent guilds, who have talked themselves into believing video-cassettes will be their biggest-ever pie in the sky, didn't like that. Two days after the unveiling, the American Federation of Musicians demanded Disco-Vision payments in its new contract for any of its members playing on the sound track of any movie sold for home use. Video residuals also figured in the 1973 writers' strike, and new labor contracts now sometimes include "extraterrestrial rights," just in case videodiscs are beamed by satellite for cable television.

The copyright question is extremely complex, and tied to what will be on the shelves of the local record shop or drugstore book section. The breakthrough year in cassette technology is expected to be 1977. Swedish economist Gunnar Bergwall has calculated it would take a player "population" of 2 million to make an original feature film viable on cassettes, but only 500,000 for "how to" programs. Others estimate that it would require at least a $50 million investment in software before any popular takeoff, but that three years after such an investment, a multibillion-dollar industry would exist.

Hollywood is the holder of the biggest dossier of copyrights (during the Golden Era more than 400 movies rolled off the studio assembly lines every year), but the majors are hesitant to commit their "vaults" to any one system (1,500 Fox films five years old or older were once "pledged" to CBS's early starter, EVR), which doesn't mean everybody isn't jockeying for position. But copyright means much more than rights to the original *Frankenstein* or *An American in Paris*. It means coming to terms with the guilds and unions—at one point in 1973, the Writers' Guild of America wanted retroactive residuals for videocassettes back to 1948! It also means rights to as-yet-unfilmed material, and although the "communications giants," RCA and CBS, pulled out of the hardware race, they are in such formidable positions in the software one that their reentry is nearly inevitable. Both own huge inventories of programming and copyrights which can quickly be put on videodiscs; both have big production staffs in their network departments (RCA *owns* NBC) that can be geared up to produce programming for the new format. The storehouse of information from years of experience in production and marketing, with their respective record and music divisions, makes them irresistible partners for MCA, a middle-sized conglomerate, and Holland's mighty Philips (Norelco in the United States). Also, both have acquired publishing houses—CBS bought Holt, Rinehart and Winston, plus four educational film production companies, and RCA acquired Random House—in order to have access to thousands of other titles.

While the giants stock up on software, while hardware makers combine sophistication with simplicity of operation, versatility, and realistic pricing, the video revolution continues "up front." Shooting on videotape has made its sharpest inroads in cost-conscious Hollywood, and developments are leapfrogging forward.

"We'll have to apologize in six months for the best jobs we do today," said Mel Sawelson of Consolidated Film Industries, which, along with Technicolor's Vidtronics subsidiary and Image Transform, handles most film and video postproduction work in Hollywood. Jack McClenahan of Trans-American Video suggested in 1973 that within eight years most big-screen features will be shot on videotape, and a year later Image Transform's Joseph Bluth ("the father of electronic photography") said he felt that within three years or less it would be possible for electronic images transferred to film stock to be blown up to fill forty-foot screens without loss of *any* quality.

Theatrical features shot on videotape can be "filmed" in seventeen days instead of the average forty-five-day schedule (half-hour TV episodes can be shot in one day instead of the two-and-a-half-day average). In 1973 Sawelson, McClenahan, and Bluth agreed that features should still be shot on film base, but a year later transfer techniques were so advanced that it was impossible to tell if a scene projected on 16-mm. stock had been filmed or taped.

Advances in lighting have eliminated the "harsh" look associated with early videotaping, and the expertise of film-oriented directors has made it possible to light a set as artistically as in any film-base movie and has also brought the single-camera style into a medium traditionally using the three-camera technique. Indeed, Hollywood video technicians now worry about artistic factors, indicating a desire to "project" the reputation of tape. "Film people who say tape is no good are ignorant," says Bluth. "Tape projects better on TV screens than film, and it is approaching the level of acceptability for big screens."

The technical obstacle has been the *transfer* from tape to film base for big-screen projection. Laser beam recorders from Philips and CBS are in use, but Image Transform's process has been the breakthrough, allowing not only a transfer but an *enhancement* of the electronic image. "In a sense, we take the electronic information apart, 'clean' it, enhance it, and put it back together again on film," says inventor John Lowry, whose process is used by the National Aeronautics and Space Administration to "enhance" Apollo moon shot tapes for television. Also, the Image Transform process allows miniaturization and "intercutting" of tape and film.

The blurring frontier has caused consternation in labor circles, where union jurisdiction is suddenly overlapping and no one really knows where one medium begins and another ends. Traditionally, IA represents film workers and NABET television technicians, but what is an Image Transform image? To remain relevant, the unions must come to grips with movies "transformed" from tape and with the loss of jobs that is inherent in the adoption of high-speed video-tape techniques.

The newest word in frontier jargon is synergy: in biology the action of two or more substances, organs, or organisms to achieve an effect of which each is individually incapable, and, in theology, regeneration through combining human will and godly grace. Minority art, each person's possession of his or her own vault of cinema classics, and do-it-yourself movies do not exhaust the possibilities for videodiscs. Other innovations will open up a whole new range of possibilities in the realm of information storage. Sooner or later, many experts believe, cable television will replace over-the-air broadcasting altogether. The opportunity will then be open for every household to be plugged into a network of cable TV data banks containing—and available to all—all material on videocassettes or discs, all books and materials in libraries and museums, and much else besides. Simple home computers will be able to retrieve material instantly for immediate presentation on the screen: a movie or, "frame by frame," a scientific article or an ancient Persian manuscript.

In this context, the entertainment industry would evolve into a "congeneracy," i.e., a communications service providing books, records, movies, radio, television, and other sources of electronic information not yet invented or just on the drawing boards. A single property, such as *The New York Times*, could be "synergized" into a multimedia endeavor extending its present newspaper, radio station, and microfilm boundaries into videocassettes, cable TV reports, and audio books, thereby creating a synergy that would derive many times the benefits (and revenue) from essentially the same corporate source. Magazines and newspapers would no longer be delivered to the door but would either be shown visually on TV or printed out in the home on a special machine. Futurologists are certain the design-it-yourself trend will soon reach books, magazines, and perhaps films. The Tokyo daily *Asahi Shimbun* has demonstrated a low-cost Telenews system for printing newspapers in the home, a first step toward the each-his-own newspaper of the future, argues Toffler—"a peculiar newspaper offering no two viewer-readers the same content."

"In the cinema, feedback is possible almost exclusively in what I call the synesthetic mode," Gene Youngblood has written, explaining that movie audiences are forced to create along with the film, to interpret for themselves what they are experiencing.[2] The video revolution *should* bring experimentation back to mainstream moviemaking. Beyond the canned conventional material, videodiscs should find a higher use as a creative medium, and people should be shooting films as casually as they now type.

Yet, relentless fracturing of audiences may not further the art of light and shadow. With all patterns becoming improvisational, including the making, distribution, and exhibition of films, and with audiences breaking into noncommunicating entities, movies might be a parody of themselves: self-indulgent playbacks of each consumer's own fantasies rather than someone else's experience absorbed for entertainment and enlightenment.

2. Gene Youngblood, *Expanded Cinema*. New York: E. P. Dutton, 1970.

15

Recycling the Movies

"THE 1960S WERE VERY DISRUPTIVE, very chaotic for the movies," director Sidney Pollack said between *The Way We Were* and *The Yakuza*. "I think tomorrow is behind us, not in a straight line, but in the middle of a knot, like a pretzel."

Pollack thinks popular demands are pulling the medium back from unstructured experimentation and radicalism, that filmgoers seem—with some exceptions—to be opting for escape rather than concern and involvement. "We're going back to the roots. The sixties have been a fantastic period, a period that opened up the movies and allowed immense gains. I think we lost our way somehow and that we're now casting about for solid ground again."

The point of popular art is not to defeat expectations but to outdo them, and the movies have always looked for the future in the past.

Trends *are* elusive, and much executive brain power is spent reading boxoffice tea leaves. It was inevitable that the Aquarian Age would respond to "tribal vibrations" on film also, but why *Easy Rider* and *Woodstock?* Roger Corman and Richard Rush had made easy flowing bike pictures before, even with Laszlo Kovacs on camera and long visually lyrical passages with rock music on the sound track, and Michael Wadleigh's *Woodstock* was by no means the first, or perhaps not even the best, of the rock festival documentaries. Why *The Odd Couple* and not *Plaza Suite?* Why *Z* and not *State of Seige?* Why *Shaft* and not *Shaft in Africa?*

If it takes a sixth sense to sniff trends before they happen, it takes X-ray prescience to know when to jump off a bandwagon. The James Bond hits *From Russia with Love* and *Goldfinger* produced sixty basement imitations (roughly in two equal subgroups: the *Spy Who Came in from the Cold* line of grubby realism and moral squalor, of frazzled, fatigued but basically decent men being obliged to betray or kill others no worse than themselves; and pictures treating international intrigue as a protext for Machiavellian farce). By the time Joseph Losey had Monica Vitti play a campy lady 007 and Dean Martin had done his second Matt Helm character sequel, anyone could see the wave was ebbing. Yet, after the Vietnam war had made Bond into a fascist pig and after Sean Connery had been unsuccessfully replaced by George Lazenby, *Live and Let Die*, with Roger Moore incarnating the secret agent, could still rack up $25 million. The black wave started with *Cotton Comes to Harlem*, and by the time of *Hell Up in Harlem* and *That Man Bolt* any shrewd producer would have felt it was time to turn down new "blaxploitation" scripts, but they were still coming, under such names as *Black the Ripper* and *The Black Godfather*, when they weren't mixing with other trends such as *The Big Zapper* (woman secret agent and kung fu martial arts) and *Black Belt Jones* and *Three the Hard Way* (kung fu and blaxploitation).

Why kung fu at all? For years Hong Kong producers like Raymond Chow and Run Run Shaw have turned out karate-kung fu movies with Chinese heroes and Japanese villains. Perhaps the answer is, as Aljean Harmetz has speculated, that "when even John Wayne can no longer be trusted to triumph with honor, something else is necessary." [1]

Emotional overloads are by no means a modern inflationary trend. The movies always aimed more at surprising than at clarifying, always tried to overwhelm rather than to elucidate, to gauge audience desires. Mother Goose platitudes have been repeated a thousand times, and the plot of almost all films from *The Great Train Robbery* on have shown virtue to triumph over wickedness and have proved that villains are powerless before little children.

The cinema lends itself to recycling, both on a mechanical level and on a deeper, almost organic stratum. Unlike books, records, and paintings, movies do not stand still and are not for sale. There

1. *Los Angeles Times*, Jan. 6, 1974.

are no residual rights if someone reads his favorite book or plays his favorite record a tenth time, but a film "belongs" to someone, and its screening is forbidden without prior consent and payment.

Hollywood always knew that the public will not remember the last time a story has been told. (Howard Hawks made the smash hit *Ball of Fire* for Samuel Goldwyn, with Gary Cooper and Barbara Stanwyck, in 1941, and Messrs. Hawks and Goldwyn remade it, shot for shot, seven years later as *A Song Is Born*, this time with Danny Kaye and Virginia Mayo.) Besides, even if audiences were to feel they had seen a story before, the original would not be available for verification. When Fox remade *Stagecoach* in 1966, with Gordon Douglas directing, it threatened to sue any theater or individual who might have a print of the John Ford original. This attitude can go to the silliest extremes. When the 1973 Tehran film festival honored the elder statesman Frank Capra, his 1937 *Lost Horizon* was quietly eliminated from the retrospective because the current version might have been hurt by comparison. Andrew Sarris has maintained that in the late 1950s only Parisian film buffs with their unique access to repertory screenings at the Cinémathèque française could have invented the *auteur* theory. A young London, New York, or Stockholm François Truffaut couldn't even see *Ball of Fire* or *A Song is Born*, and older critics simply relied on memory about "middle period" Hawks. Television has helped somewhat, but no thirty- or even fifty-year-old movie can be borrowed from anyone's neighborhood library, let alone be purchased in anything but a surreal 16-mm. black market. The fringe of the industry is peopled with a few unsavory characters who specialize in seeking out widows of pioneers and, for a pittance, making them sign over copyrights. The result is that the handful of American collectors of classics live in constant fear of lawsuits and must be careful about who they invite to private screenings in their own basements.

Even if latter-day cowpokes kiss gals instead of horses, there are supposedly only five possible plots of *any* western. A "horse opera" is a story about mortgages, land rights, crooked politicians, stagecoach and/or train robberies, or smuggling, or it is a combination of any or several of these ingredients. Any year's Ten Best, it seems, will include a strange, severe, and beautiful western (alternating in odd years with a funny, anarchic western), a film about small-town adolescence, a cunning escape vehicle, etc. Not only are plots redundant and characters cardboard-thin in B and Z movies, but sophisticated *oeuvres* like Mike Nichols' *The Day of the Dolphin* can reduce the story of a scientist's growing moral and political responsibility to Rin Tin Tin pulp. Creators and performers constantly trade on their fame and past success. For the debut of a "new" Julie Andrews television show, she will dish up her Cole Porter–*My Fair Lady*–*Mary Poppins* repertoire, and George Roy Hill, Paul Newman, and Robert Redford will trade again and again on *Butch Cassidy and the Sundance Kid*. Vilmos Zsigmond will be asked to *repeat* his sepia cinematography, and Francis Lai will be imported to rewrite his *Un Homme et une Femme* resonances in a *Love Story* score. Fame, *any* fame, is negotiable.

This recycling of material and individual success is favored by the nature of the beast. Popular cinema deals in particularized emotions, but its preference is for generalized facts.

The Indians may cut off the U.S. cavalry at the pass in modern epics and cops may actually be robbers, but the lines of conflict are as clear-cut as in any 1905 two-reeler. Traitors abound, but there are always *sides* to betray or doublecross. If the hero is a convicted murderer, like Papillon, then guards are brutes and prisoners either nice guys or people doing time for bad raps. If he is Alex in *A Clockwork Orange*, then everybody around him becomes dirty authority figures, a deformed and hypocritical establishment.

The French Connection is exemplary moviemaking: clean lines of conflict, good guys, bad guys (detectives and dope pushers), and a pulsating chase. As directed by William Friedkin, the film is a triumph of strong, seductive screenfare and visual engineering (which its producer, Phil d'Antoni, failed to match in his directorial debut, *The Seven-Ups*). The good guy–bad guy dichotomy can be switched but not blurred without loss of incandescence. The hero of *Super Fly* is a cocaine pusher, but his outlawry is then shown as a triumph over ghetto conditions, a way out to beat white oppression. The only "dope pictures" that failed were films that couldn't make up their minds whether narcotics were hip or a social plague, i.e., whether narcotics agents were fascist pigs or society's last-stand heroes on the sleaziest of frontiers.

It is extraordinarily difficult to do conflictless narratives on the screen (comedy and musicals are no exception). Other outer limits are the portrayal of goodness, sports, and metaphysics, and the showing of thought in progress rather than action in motion.

Film history is littered with stubborn attempts at depicting good people, ambivalent personality, and expanded consciousness. Modern films are "contemporary" in their psychological affectations, their cultural cynicism, and their intuitive surfaces of flare, texture, and tone, but even the screen's masters have all the difficulty in the world penetrating the deeper maze of modern sensibility. Despite singular attempts by Michelangelo Antonioni, Ingmar Bergman, and Luis Buñuel at splashing spiritual values, ambiguity, and narrative overtones on the screen, such inflamed areas of contemporary catharsis as the supernatural and the visionary, myth, and inner-direction are virtually untouched territory.

Besides such obvious taboos as old age, renunciation, and numbing melancholy, the screen has practically never treated love founded in an adult relationship or based on the equality of partners. Buñuel's *La Voie Lactée* ("The Milky Way") is the only theological thriller in film history and Carl Dryer's *Gertrud* the only movie about elegiac sadness. The movies somehow don't take kindly to burning radicals, tormented moralists, or holy men.

What also helps the cinema recycle itself is its penchant for nostalgia. "The flashback in the forties and fifties was not really a narrative device at all but a compulsion, the instrument of a constant, eager plunging into the past," Michael Wood has written. "A slow, misty dissolve and off we went into the day before yesterday when things were different; into a time before all this (whatever *all this* might be in any given movie) happened to us." [2]

Movies work as sensory feedback, as mirrored images. They are very good at treating tension and intense naturalism, and at sentimentalizing clouded innocence. The better screen artists can transmute trivia into pertinent metaphor, externalize some matters of the mind, strike contemporary nerves, and create atmospheres for living. Among the special graces of the movies, Arthur Penn has asserted, is the number of bells of recognition they ring in audiences' consciences, and how *true* they ring.

If the cinema had always thrived on stories about criminals, outlaws, fallen women, and other sentimentalized views of life on the seamy side, it has matured on its own echoes. *Casablanca* is not only Humphrey Bogart in black-and-white backlot Morocco with Ingrid Bergman and Claude Rains, it's a whole association of

2. *New York Review of Books*, Nov. 29, 1973.

images and evocative personal responses. Layers of recognition pile up in audiences and can become screen material in their turn. Robert Altman's *The Long Goodbye* feeds not only on the earlier celluloid lives of Raymond Chandler's private eye, but on the interspace between them. As fleshed out by Elliott Gould, Philip Marlowe has none of Bogart's romantic machismo or Robert Montgomery's clenched-teeth delivery, but is a crazy sweet innocent saddled with obsolete values and struggling to survive in a tawdry, movie-influenced L.A.

When released on the West Coast during the winter of 1972–73, *The Long Goodbye* was accused of being a sacrilegious desecration of its Chandlerian source. It opened to largely negative reviews (*Variety:* "an uneven mixture of insider satire on the gumshoe film genre, gratuitous brutality, and sledgehammer whimsy") and quickly disappeared, its demise further hastened by uninspired ads and bookings. Ten months later Pauline Kael gave it an electrifying review, leading to an unprecedented "second chance" rerelease.

Filmmakers have constantly extended their language to isolate and confirm feelings that previously were only thin air. Acute change has always been endemic to the cinema, and it can be argued that as an art form film matured in a state of permanent instability.

It *is* late in the movies. It was on Saturday, December 20, 1895, that the Lumière brothers first threw a moving picture onto a white sheet and got money for it. It was on Friday, August 2, 1926, that the movies learned to talk. The public first deserted the medium in 1907 when the initial flush of interest waned. The year 1915 saw the convulsive breakup of the Motion Picture Patent Company, 1923 witnessed the first massive layoffs in Hollywood. Warner Brothers was on the verge of collapse in 1927 and Paramount went into bankruptcy in 1933. Movie attendance nosedived in 1948, and because of wide-screen developments, 1953 was billed the year of the great transition. Between 1971 and '73, the majors totaled losses of more than half a billion dollars.

Between 1915 and 1960, the cinema was a monopoly with a handful of absolute monarchs lording over world empires, but Hollywood's classical age actually spanned no more than fifteen years—1933 to 1948, roughly. In 1953 *Gone with the Wind* producer David Selznick could already tell Ben Hecht that Hollywood was like Egypt, "full of crumbled pyramids."

Screenfare is its own diminishing returns. Shortly before his one hundredth birthday, Paramount's founding father, Adolph Zukor, said it with admirable simplicity: "In the beginning, motion pictures were a novelty and it made no difference what you showed on the screen. The number of subjects that can bring the public into theaters is getting less."

Examining the 1908 "crisis of the subject," the late Georges Sadoul has written that the movies barely knew how to tell a story when they plunged into psychology, complex plot lines, and subjects adapted from history and classical theater. "Everything was hurriedly put together in ten minutes' screen time with poor means and expressed in a primitive filmic language. 'The mania with which these two-reelers imitated each other exhausted the public further,' critics wrote at the time, 'made the public weary of disheveled chases with wet nurses, legless cripples, and gendarmes, of the flash melodramas where a countess marries, loses her child, tries to drown herself, is rescued by a bearded mountaineer, and, after eighteen years, finds her daughter again, recognizing her through the laundry markings on her clothes. The cinema lacked imagination." [3]

The imminent demise of Hollywood was first forecast in 1914. In the late 1920s critics, directors, and esthetes all agreed with Mary Pickford that grafting dialogue on films was "like putting lip rouge on the Venus of Milo." In the late 1940s, *Life* predicted the advent of television would witness among the Hollywood ruins "the bleached bones of some $4,000 a-week executives who, incredulous to the last, died miserably of malnutrition of body and ego." Twenty years later, Hollywood was earning a quarter of its domestic revenue from the tube.

The 1960s *were* disruptive. The 1950s had dragged on too long and too boringly, but by 1965 even Hollywood had caught on to other times, other moods and values and critical assumptions. The impetus of the sixties was not Hollywoodian, but European, and the readjustment was painful in creativity and in exploring new themes as well as in the skilled use of the afterglow of past Hollywood glories. Michelangelo Antonioni's *La Notte*, Tony Richardson's *A Taste of Honey*, Luis Buñuel's *Viridiana*, John Cassavetes' New York "underground" *Shadows*, and François Truffaut's *Shoot the Piano Player* were appreciated and envied by Hollywood's elder

3. Georges Sadoul, *Histoire du Cinéma Mondial*. Paris: Flammarion, 1949.

statesman. The Truffaut, Richardson, and Cassavetes works were studied for their fresh, spontaneous realism. Truffaut scrambled comedy, pathos, and tragedy, something usually avoided in Hollywood filmmaking, and Richardson also went against the Hollywood directors' tendency to drive points home and to "point up" climaxes. *Viridiana* and Buñuel's other goading parables disturbed, while *La Notte* and Antonioni's other probes of the relations between the sexes were admired for the very thinness of the subject matter and the cinematic power used to express it, for the narrative structure designed not so much to advance the plot as to bring out certain meanings. Some Hollywood directors derided the "new cinema," but many saw the writing on the wall. As the 1960s marched on, Hollywood felt obliged to pay more than lip service to cinema of "personal expression."

Agonizing reappraisals were not only confined to Southern California dream factories. The movies moved fast everywhere. The French New Wave fell from grace following successive fizzles, the Russian cinema sought ways to catch up with the times in story material without opening the floodgates of "revisionism," the Italian film industry remained a handful of individuals towering over a sea of Neapolitan pasta, and the impetus of England's second Elizabethan Age expressed itself in rock music and fashion, not in a movie renaissance.

The dwindling attendance around the world explains a good deal of what has happened in the movies. To retain the audiences, Hollywood made them bigger. Sometimes it worked. (The incredible *Sound of Music*, together with *Doctor Zhivago, Mary Poppins, My Fair Lady*, and *Funny Girl*, earned upwards of half a billion dollars worldwide.) Sometimes it didn't. *Mutiny on the Bounty* nearly ruined MGM, and *Star!, Dr. Dolittle*, and *Hello, Dolly!* were disastrous for the Darryl Zanuck regime at Fox.

Meanwhile, the vast market of teen-agers and young adults remained largely indifferent to the movies until Mike Nichols' *The Graduate* came along in 1968 (which in the United States and Canada alone grossed $43 million in two years). A year earlier, Arthur Penn had created a key film with *Bonnie and Clyde*, elevating a pair of sleazy thirties robbers to national heroes, and the year's Oscar went to Norman Jewison's *In the Heat of the Night*, another film that was to spawn a whole genre of movies about cops. Then in 1969,

Dennis Hopper's *Easy Rider* hit Hollywood the way Volkswagen hit Detroit. Shot on a starvation budget of $400,000, the lyrical hymn to a generation grossed $30 million.

The flop percentage is the same for little movies as for superproductions, but the big-money losers hurt more. In 1970 they forced the majors to call a series of temporary production halts to take stock of where their extraordinary industry stood.

The *Easy Rider* belt tightened around the necks of prima-donna producers and directors with a record of bringing pictures in late and over budget. Retrenchment was the order of the day. Five years later, the trend was reversed. Buoyed by the boxoffice returns of big-budget "multiple jeopardy" films—movies in the *Poseidon Adventure, Towering Inferno, Airport 1975, Hindenburg* vein offering their audiences shared peril of natural or man-made disasters —again put corporate Hollywood in the expansive mood.

The media game, however, is always to write Hollywood-sinking-into-its-own-sunset obituaries—even while claiming the world is on the threshold of a video revolution. What the Hollywood-is-dead obit writers rarely mention is that (1) if fewer films are made, the reason is *also* that movies are getting more playing time (regardless of quality, a 1930s theater manager changed the playbill twice a week); (2) the winners are making more money than ever (*The Godfather* and *The French Connection* earned more than a whole studio's former annual income); and (3) cost control and streamlined operations are an indication of industrial health, not terminal cancer. The Hollywood financial structure is today based on corporate equity, which means the industry is more than ever in the business of making movies instead of hunting for bank loans.

Nor do the Cassandras mention that Hollywood's batting average, bad as it is, is better than that of other consumer arts. A book selling 100,000 copies is a runaway best seller; modern dance and ballet attendance is said to have "exploded" in recent years because 8 million Americans are in the audience; and classical music is thought to be enjoying a boom because 11 million people go to concerts every year. But more than 900 million movie tickets are sold yearly across the United States. Even if only one film out of four makes a profit, the Hollywood "scores" are still ten times those of Broadway's hits.

Weekly movie admissions have been sliding for a quarter of a century—from a peak somewhere around 80 million in 1946.[4] By 1963 the weekly total was down to 21 million, to stabilize in 1970 at around 15 to 18 million. The phenomenon is worldwide, except in Taiwan, India, and the Soviet Union. During the past twenty years, film attendance has declined 70 percent in Japan, 80 percent in Germany, and 85 percent in Great Britain.[5]

Yet the film industry is still hanging in there, skidding about on the uncertain slopes of popular tastes, guessing and dodging, scanning the heavens for the lodestar of "entertainment," recycling its best past and adapting to an audience of growing sophistication. "There are a lot of interesting, good people around," *Newsweek* quoted Pauline Kael as saying in a special issue on the arts in America. "If they get a chance to work, it's going to be a great period in American movies—that is, if it stays chaotic long enough. As long as businessmen control the movies, the artist's only hope is chaos." [6]

4. The 80-million weekly admission figure is tentative, and usually advanced by the Motion Picture Producers' Association. Box office receipts always fluctuate radically from season to season, even from week to week, so any "average" figure is pertinent only in an abstract sense.

5. According to *Encyclopedia Britannica*, the world's highest per capita attendance is in Taiwan (66 percent), Hong Kong (21 percent), the U.S.S.R. (19 percent), and British Honduras (18 percent).

6. *Newsweek*, Dec. 24, 1973.

16

Good Guys Do Finish First

THE MOVIES have always lived as if there were no tomorrow, and no yesterday. The cinema is a service industry—a commodity for a mass society and a mirror of popular demands for insights and ecstasy. Like the other arts in America, the movies produce both money and a need for money. With television taking over the burden of being all things to all people, the movies have achieved, at least theoretically, almost unlimited freedom.

With the most fascinating story material in front of their noses, with more elbow room than ever, and with audiences and rewards progressing, American filmmakers seem to have no other limitations than themselves. But the movies are an emotional business. The climb is unpredictable, and the room at the top tenuous. Making it, Andrew Sarris has written, means Making a Living, Making a Killing, and Making a Life. "For many, Making a Life becomes an objective too late in life to save the overextended ego from its excesses."

In a glass house like the film industry, with its built-in glare, its massive inadvertencies and trendy obsessions, hanging on to a career is in itself an art. The shoals to avoid are, on one hand, being above, ahead of, or behind popular yearnings and, on the other, making undue compromises to protect commercial success. By temperament the movies are not political, and the conscious use of the screen for ends extraneous to film is perhaps as self-defeating as mindless attempts at making everybody a little happy all the time.

"Directors who say films are an art have either been extremely lucky or they are utter fools," says a member of the profession, John Frankenheimer.

If we only hear about "hot" people, it is because the "cold" people tend to disappear, not only because they are thrust out of the limelight but because they themselves slink off. Failure is humiliating. The only thing Hollywood—and, ultimately, the American psyche—trusts is success.

But success itself is open-ended, tentative, and perishable. The trap for consumer artists who come to epitomize their "generation"—and these very "with it" people are precisely what the cinema demands—is that when the age they reflect goes down, so do they. Whom the gods wish to destroy, they first make fashionable.

The films that a few years ago catered to the grossest fantasies of the youth cult look as dated today as the regulated fantasies of the Fabulous Forties. Likewise, opting for cynical escape rather than concern and involvement must be equally ephemeral. It takes no great amount of wisdom to see that sadistic murderers, corrupt lawmen, and wiped-out people cannot forever appeal to large audiences any more than lacerating, numbing, and self-conscious *auteurist* movies on alienation and anomie. Big, romantic screen fantasies with big, incandescent stars are, of necessity, a movie staple.

Popular arts always thrive on folk myths, and James Bond and John Shaft belong to the same misty world of gods and goddesses, monsters and usurpers, as the knight who after slaying the dragon marries the princess and gets half the kingdom. Heroes are always admired, and they are always brave and resourceful. The perils of the plot are designed to measure their strength—exile, slavery, and attempted seduction by the villain's mistress are obstacles everybody from Ulysses to Serpico have had to overcome. What is astonishing is not that the movies feed on themselves but that so little has been done to renew the diet. The filmmaker's severest limitation is content, what *can* be made.

The film industry is confronted with a perpetual chicken-and-egg situation. To live it needs a public, and for people to go to the movies the playbill must be worth it. The films that are successful are those that honor certain traditional movie virtues, films that engross their audiences with conflict, suspense, and the possibility of identification. The chase after an audience forces filmmakers, even successful *auteurs*, to pick story material with a "certain low cunning," story material that appeals to the very young who form the bulk of moviegoers. But catering to this narrow wedge of the public also tends to make moviegoing a habit most people outgrow. If the movies have lost the over-thirty audience, it is also because they have little to say to adults, because it is difficult to "grow" with a medium that likes to recycle itself. Artistic growth traditionally has meant transcending, daring not to please, but a certain shallowness is built into mass culture.

"I like, when I go to the cinema, to see something of the person who made it there, I want a human experience of some sort," said John Schlesinger while filming Nathanael West's *The Day of the Locust*. "There's no such thing as a simple success story."

Growth in Hollywood is also knowing when and how to fight success.

The question whose answer remains elusive is, What *is* the public "out there" really like? Movie audiences are perhaps less a pie that can be cut up in so many ways than a well of unknown depth and capacity. There is a body of opinion which believes conventions are still in working order and that audiences have never changed, that moviemakers foolishly surrendered to the critics who insisted the audience *had* changed. Conventional industry wisdom has it that people go to the movies to get away from it all, and there is a "yo-yo" theory saying that films are the opposite of where society is at: Depressing and confusing times demand tranquilizing escapism, and good times respond to realism and inner probes.

The money chase has given audiences veto power. Whether added up in dollars or bodies, film is first and foremost a matter of numbers. Lately, however, there is talk of moviegoers getting the screenfare they ultimately deserve. By being lazy and undemanding, it is said, audiences share the responsibility for what ends up on the screen. This kind of thinking is positively revolutionary in a medium where the client has always been right.

But, object emerging talents, all American cinema is not Hollywoodian. Yes and no. Scores of features are, of course, made in New York and elsewhere every year, but insofar as getting a film to market means coming to terms with one of the majors, all American moviemaking obeys mainstream habits developed during half a century of commercial rules. The artists' uneasiness when facing the industry is natural, but, as in the other arts in America, movies are also packagers, distributors, consumers, and not always fully understood connections.

The distinction between "good" films and commercial films is now more obscure than ever. To equate noncommercial movies with "good" movies is as silly as to say that commercial films are inartistic. Low-budget movies don't necessarily attract audiences, not even their *intended* audiences, and cinematic *auteur*-ship is not only artistic imagination. As Truffaut showed in *Day for Night*, making a movie is a hassle from beginning to end. It also demands creative authority.

The limits of filmmaking, American-style, are inherent and obvious. In the United States, the cinema must obey the laws of the marketplace. Although the idea of the U.S. government doling out grants to the Los Angeles film factories still seems somewhat farfetched, the notion that film is an amenity for which the state holds itself partially responsible, like public libraries and playgrounds, is looking less and less preposterous. Pleading in the French National Assembly for a government film subsidy, André Malraux remarked in 1964 that "even if the cinema must earn money, it is not essential that *every* film should do so." Ten years later, Washington was spending $60 million a year on the arts, and state and local governments another $40 million, and—more important to the film industry—the U.S. Supreme Court upheld a claim for federal income tax credits, amounting, in effect, to a one-shot film subsidy of nearly 10 percent.

"Will There Ever Be a 21st Century–Fox?" *Time* headlined a 1970 story detailing Hollywood's economic debacle that year. Five years later, the movies and the people who make them enjoyed a string of hits. In terms of financial health, the industry has never looked better than today. The majors have suffered and slimmed and are now back making pictures and profits.

The only trend in the mid-seventies, it seems, is that there is no trend at all. Youth-market bonanzas are now few and far between, sex is a risky boxoffice magnet, and violence has become the victim of its own on-screen overkill. Yet the films that perform worst with the public are those coming from what *Variety* once called the "standard mixmasters, the kind of films that suspicious critics think are programmed on a computer." Today's smart money rides once again on stars and the handful of name directors who have proved consistently reliable. But smart money also backs movies that break away from conventional molds and movies that successfully return to certainties. In fact, smart money will ride on anything that reflects the shifts in contemporary sensibilities, perception, and awareness, and therefore will mirror current hungers, yearnings, truths, and fantasies.

"It is hard to laugh at the need for beauty and romance," Nathanael West wrote in his Hollywood novel *The Day of the Locust*, "no matter how tasteless, even horrible, the results of that are. But it is easy to sigh. Few things are sadder than the truly monstrous."

This all makes for wide-open opportunities for both charlatans and quasi-artists, and it makes for soul-searching in executive suites and Bel Air screening rooms. Nobody really knows what goes and what doesn't, and that helps both filmmakers who see movies as expressing the on-going, organic life of society and those who believe in creative chaos and art as protean conflict.

Marshall McLuhan has said that we live in a time of provisional judgment. Nowhere is it truer, perhaps, that in the mirror art called the movies.

Acknowledgments

I wish to express my gratitude to The Academy of Motion Picture Arts and Sciences.

I wish to thank *Variety*'s Art Murphy for repeating what to him is obvious, and Yale Udoff for editorial advice.

Index